A LOAD OF OLD BALLS

Men in History

Jo Brand

SIMON & SCHUSTER
LONDON SYDNEY NEW YORK TOKYO SINGAPORE TORONTO

First published in Great Britain by Simon & Schuster Ltd, 1994.
A Paramount Communications Company

Simon & Schuster
West Garden Place
Kendal Street
London W2 2AQ

Simon & Schuster of Australia Pty Ltd
Sydney

A CIP catalogue record for this book is available from the British Library
ISBN 0–671–71385–X

Designed & produced by Harrington & Co 130 Kingsland Road London E2 8DP

Printed in Great Britain by
The Bath Press

All photographs copyright of The Hulton Deutsch Collection except,
Take That pages 151–156 and Sid Vicious pages 15–20 copyright London Features,
George Orwell page 351 copyright Popperfoto
and pages 349 and 354 copyright Camera Press.

Contents

Introduction

Throughout history, lots of famous and respected men have managed to hide the more unsavoury side of their characters. In fact, the further back you go, the nicer they seem, because time always makes raping and pillaging easier to deal with. We've all sat in history lessons at primary school thinking 'Well I suppose that Oliver Cromwell's all right then,' because we are taught only the bare facts, not the seedy details. If history books went into more detail about the character and relationships of the people we study, they would be a lot more exciting.

Many of the more powerful men in history were either mad, horrible or endowed with a personality that would put you off meeting them in a dark alley. The achievements they tend to be admired for involve lots of killings and not much flower arranging. In nine out of ten cases, the boy who made it was the school bully rather than the speccy herbert who sat in the corner and liked animals.

Through the centuries, women have had to sit back and take it, without being allowed to get a word in edgeways. We have been decorative, child-producing pieces of furniture, occasionally called upon to knock up an apple pie, hardly ever getting a chance to upset things. (Apart from royal women, who, most of the time, behaved just like men in order to keep up with them.)

In this book I have looked at a few of the old bastards scattered through history. Not all the blokes in this book are horrible, however, some of them are quite nice. Contrary to the opinion of a few gorilla look-alikes, I am not a man-hater at all, in fact I think men are fantastic...as a concept. It's just the reality of their behaviour that's the problem. There are also a few contemporary characters thrown in to spice it up a bit and keep me busy in court for a few years. Much as I would have liked to, I was advised against including a section on Muhammed unless I wanted to go and live with Salman Rushdie for a few years.

This is not a book anyone should use to study for their History GCSE. Well, not unless they want to end up failing.

I'd like to say I enjoyed writing this book but I am a very lazy person and am now suffering from Repetitive Strain Injury, which is making it difficult for me to eat my dinner and smoke my usual 80 fags a day.

I'd like to thank Pat Condell, Jez Feeney and Jim Miller for their help in getting this book together. I apologise for not having asked any girls to help but, as you know, they are all too busy reading *Woman's Own* or waxing their bikini-lines. I hope you enjoy it and get a few laughs out of it.

HENRY VIII

(Tudor)

The last really pokable bloke in England

'I can't move in this girdle'

Henry VIII, or King Syphilis Gut Bucket Wife Murderer VIII as I prefer to call him, was born in 1491 and, despite all the paintings we know and love of him looking like a great big beached whale, he was quite athletic as a young man. At the age of 18 his brother Arthur died and Henry married his widow, Catherine of Aragon.

Henry was always an ambitious young man and he thought it best to get the male heir business out of the way before he set off on conquering expeditions. There must have been something dodgy as far as the royal sperm was concerned because it took bloody ages. Henry always had a bit of an inferiority complex, being the second son, and he grew up to be an egotistical, self-righteous, cruel man – in fact, the last sort of person who should have been King. I often wonder when I read English history why so many of the royals were such vicious bastards and I think it's probably because they could be. Give our Queen half a chance and she'd be up The Mall with a crossbow picking off Japanese tourists and nicking their cameras.

Catherine of Aragon had five children but only one of them survived and unfortunately, as far as Henry was concerned, that one was useless. Mentally handicapped? Physically disabled? Well, in Tudor-think, both: she was a girl. They were together for nearly twenty years but, when Catherine began to get hot flushes and started doing a bit of shoplifting, Henry realised she would not be able to have any more children and, like a dutiful loving husband, he told Catherine not to worry and that everything would be all right. Did he fuck. He did his utmost to get rid of her without actually bumping her off.

Because Henry had already had to get a special dispensation from the Pope to marry Catherine, it didn't look good for another favour from the Catholic Church. In fact, as far as the Pope was concerned, he had as much chance of getting a divorce as he did of winning a Gary Lineker look-alike contest. So Henry decided, rather than muck about going through the legal channels of the Catholic Church, he might as well dump them altogether and start his own little Church. So he became head of the Church in England. Nice work if you can get it. At this point he was having a good old flirt with Anne Boleyn who would not give in to his

4

'Henry then moved on to Anne of Cleves whom he charmingly named the "Flemish Mare". Pity she didn't kick him in the "Hampton Courts"'

advances unless he agreed to marry her. He did, got her up the duff, and they got married secretly. By this time Henry was pretty portly, so it was difficult for him to do anything secretly. Unfortunately Anne Boleyn did not have a son either. 'Oh, drat,' she must have thought, as the future Elizabeth I popped out. But Henry, by this stage, started to go a bit bonkers. He must have thought to himself, 'Well, I'm head of the Church, I can do what I like now.' He found some poor bloke who worked in the court, accused him of having an affair with Anne Boleyn, tortured him until he said 'Yes', and then had her executed. A bit over the top. He could just have asked her to move out.

In fact, Henry got rid of anyone in his way. He was a sort of fat, royal combine harvester. Once he was head of the Church he nicked all their money, destroyed many monasteries... Anyone who got in his way was disembowelled.

After Anne Boleyn, Henry moved on to Jane Seymour who was said to be homely and sweet. She managed to squeeze a boy child out of her womb for which she must have got down on her knees and thanked God for allowing her to continue wearing a nice selection of hats. Unfortunately (and I suppose this is the way life goes) she died 12 days later. Henry then moved on to Anne of Cleves, whom he charmingly named the 'Flemish Mare'. Pity she didn't kick him in the 'Hampton Courts'. Their marriage was never consummated...she was lucky. They divorced. He then moved on to Catherine Howard who was described by one book I read as 'a spirited minx'. More a reflection on the writer than Catherine Howard, I would have thought. She was accused of adultery and had her head chopped off as well.

Jo Brand – A Load of Old Balls

Finally, Henry finished up with Catherine Parr, who is described as amiable. In men's speak that means nice but ugly. But judging by Henry's record up to this point, it seemed safer to be not that great looking. At least you got to hang on to your bonce.

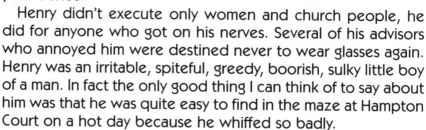

Henry didn't execute only women and church people, he did for anyone who got on his nerves. Several of his advisors who annoyed him were destined never to wear glasses again. Henry was an irritable, spiteful, greedy, boorish, sulky little boy of a man. In fact the only good thing I can think of to say about him was that he was quite easy to find in the maze at Hampton Court on a hot day because he whiffed so badly.

Legend has it that after Henry died, his body was brought back to London and it was so riddled with disease that it exploded. This has since been known, as he was a big man, as a twenty-one-gut salute.

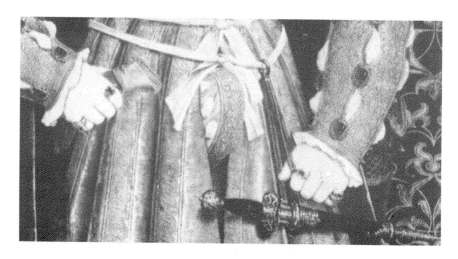

WINSTON
Churchill

To relax, Winston liked to get his kit off and stretch out on the large map on the War Cabinet Desk

*Churchill and mates watch an episode of
'That's Showbusiness'*

inston Churchill was born in 1874, the son of Lord Randolph and Jenny, a stunning American beauty, so I don't suppose many people said, 'Ooh, isn't he like his mum?' Because Churchill's family was upper class, his parents' motto was, 'Little children shouldn't be seen, or heard either,' so he was cared for by Nanny Everest, who on her days off spent time selling double glazing or being climbed by Chris Bonnington. Winston saw little of his mother, whom he adored, and sent pleading letters from boarding school begging for attention. She ignored many of these. I expect that was because for some beautiful women it is a full-time job staying pretty and you can do without the minor irritations of children pestering you.

At Harrow Winston was seen as pretty thick, and his father decided to start him, appropriately, on an army career. To get into the army in those days you just had to be able to write your own name (and not even in joined-up writing). He also worked as a journalist at this time, which he excelled at for the same reason.

He resigned his commission in 1899 and reported on the Boer War for the *Morning Post*. He became famous for rescuing an armoured train from the Boers (who hasn't?) and for escaping from one of their prison camps. This was a fair achievement as they didn't have Group Four in those days. As a popular hero Churchill won the 1900 Oldham election as a Conservative. After reading a book about the poor in York, he denounced such conditions as 'terrible and shocking'. He would have gone to look at the conditions for himself but he was too busy playing polo. But in 1906 he crossed to the Liberals over economic policy and not being able to decide whether to wear blue socks or yellow ones. One problem that may have hindered his political career was that Churchill had a slight lisp, so he used to walk up and down with one of his girlfriends, Muriel Wilson, repeating the phrase, 'The Spanish ships I cannot see for they are not in sight'. Later he proposed to Muriel but she turned him down. I'm not surprised. She must have been frustrated beyond belief.

MURIEL: Come to bed, darling.

WINSTON: The Spanish ships I cannot see for they are not in sight.

MURIEL: Oh, piss off then.

Winston Churchill travelled a lot and wrote books about his travels. After a journey in Africa he wrote a book called *My African Journey*. Blimey! He must have sweated for

'I'd have punched him in the gob'

hours over that title. In the book he reminds readers that Africa has 'poisonous reptiles and pest-spreading insects and terrible beasts of prey'. I think he got muddled here and intended this to be part of a book called *My Years in the Tory Party*.

During this period Churchill was a radical, establishing the eight-hour bill for the mines and attempting to reduce unemployment by setting up labour exchanges. However, when he became Home Secretary in 1910 he used the military against the dockers and railwaymen, so he was a bit of a wolf in creep's clothing.

As First Lord of the Admiralty from 1911 Churchill presided over the modernisation of the navy and Lloyd George said of him, 'You have become a water creature.' I'd have punched him in the gob. In the war Churchill took the blame for the disastrous Gallipoli campaign. If you want to know about this, watch the film Gallipoli, which has the added bonus of Mel Gibson in it for women whose brains don't function unless

'What does he mean: "The Spanish see, I cannot shit"??'

11

'There have been many calls in the press for me to slim down and wear a pretty dress. Dream on, tabloids'

they can see someone with big pectorals and a sexy smile.

Churchill resigned from the government in 1915, returning to the army. The food was probably a bit crap, because in 1916 he was back in parliament, and in 1917 back in the government. At this point he seemed to be moving further and further to the right. He was against votes for women and said after they had been given the vote that he would not have been so vehemently opposed if he had known so many women would vote for him. And that I'm afraid is a sad fact about women in this country: politically, they do tend to be big Tory voters, probably because they don't think about politics much. 'Civil war in former Yugoslavia? That's not going to get the washing-up done or the beds made, is it?' When the Lloyd George coalition collapsed, Winston was a casualty, and was out of parliament in 1922. When he returned in 1924, he had switched back to the Tories, as MP for Epping, and soon as Chancellor of the Exchequer. Nice to see that he remained as faithful to his political roots as Prince Charles has to his missus. Poor old Di. Charlie's spent more time talking to his cheese plant than he has to her. Then again the cheese plant's probably got more to say for itself.

Churchill had by now moved so far from his early radicalism that he was at the forefront of the opposition to the miners, editing the chauvinist and provocative *British Gazette*, a sort of early BNP mag with not quite such a short haircut. It was at this time that, obsessed by the threat of Bolshevism, he paid his famous compliments to the Mussolini regime, compliments like, 'Mm! What a lovely black shirt you're wearing!'

Between 1929 and 1939 Churchill was in the political wilderness, or until? the Tories got together with Baldwin's Labour government. With little else to think about, Churchill began to get obsessed with the threat of Nazi Germany but people thought he was crying wolf. Just after war broke out, Churchill was made Prime Minister. He was then able to go round sticking up two fingers at everyone saying,'I told you so.' Thankfully one of his advisors made sure he turned his fingers round the other way when he was giving a speech on victory. The newspapers were satisfied as there had been many calls in the press for him to be included in the government. There have been many calls in the press for me to slim down and wear a pretty dress. Dream on, tabloids.

Churchill then began his great campaign against the Nazis and no one seemed to mind that he couldn't pronounce it properly. Nartzis or Narzees, they were still evil. Churchill made many very famous speeches during the war to rouse the British people to action and courage, including the immortal words, 'We will fight them on the beaches,' a cry which has been taken up with the greatest enthusiasm by British tourists on the Costa del Sol, not as a response to the Germans invading Poland but to them putting their towels down in the best spots. These Britons are all called Shane and are functioning at the evolutionary level of an Abyssinian guinea-pig.

As country after country collapsed under the onslaught of the German army, brave Blighty stood firm under the chilling bombardment of the German Air Force! (I could get a job

Under rationing, even Winnie had to cut his Shredded Wheat consumption

Jo Brand – A Load of Old Balls

on *Combat Weekly* with prose like that.)

One problem Churchill had was trying to persuade the Americans to come into the war. Churchill visited Roosevelt and talked him into it, probably by repeating 'The Spanish ships' *ad nauseam* until Roosevelt gave in. Churchill also made friends with Stalin and the Russians, conveniently forgetting all his earlier paranoid ideas about the Bolshies.

Well, obviously you know we won the war and, if you don't, you're a serious thicko. The British voted for the Labour Party in the election at the end of it and Churchill was ousted. So he decided to get paranoid again and went stomping off round Europe and the US and invented the phrase 'the Iron Curtain'. He also wrote his memoirs and became PM again in 1951 until 1955.

Lots of people disagree about Churchill. Some think he is the biggest hero of the twentieth century and others think he was just a charismatic weirdo. Legend has it that he drank a glass of his own urine every day. Could have been worse, could have been Diet Coke. And that's the one thing Winston and I have in common... neither of us has touched the stuff.

Winston is caught cheating at the 1945 United Nations Entrance Exam

SID
Vicious

*Never mind the Boiled Socks
here's Sid and Nancy*

Sid prepares to cover his shoes with diced carrots

nce upon a time there was a little boy called Simon Beverly and he dreamed that when he grew up he would spit at people and never have a bath. When he did grow up, his dream came true, because a magic fairy arranged for him to be in a band called The Sex Pistols.

The Sex Pistols lived in a fairyland called Out Of Your Head On Drugs And Booze and they invited many young people to come and live in this land with them. They would hold big meetings called gigs when everyone would come along wearing strange clothes and bits of metal stuck through parts of their faces and do a funny dance called pogo-ing when you jumped up and down and tried to break people's glasses.

All these people who lived in Out Of Your Head land were called punks and they had their own special language which involved the use of phrases like 'Fuck off you tosser', particularly if they liked someone.

'they had their own special language which involved the use of phrases like "Fuck off you tosser", particularly if they liked someone'

Most of the young people who came to this magical land were only temporary passport holders. They were nice middle-class children really, who thought they would be allowed in if they had a safety pin on their trousers. Besides, they only wanted to join for a bit to annoy their parents and then they'd get a proper job. But they all looked up to The Sex Pistols who lived the real punk life and they wished they could be like them.

The Sex Pistols were very brave. They went on television and said 'Shit' in front of millions of tea-time viewers and showed the wicked middle-aged presenter Bill Grundy that they meant business.

Little Simon Beverly changed his name to Sid Vicious to make himself seem more scary and he went to Paris to sing some songs and upset Parisians in the Jewish quarter by wearing a T-shirt with a swastika on it. The Parisians didn't realise that Sid was really a nice boy called Simon who was just trying to be different.

One thing the real people of punk liked doing was having a fight. Sid had lots of fights with someone called Malcolm McClaren who, although he said he was a good friend of the punks, made lots of trips into the real world to check his bank balance.

The Sex Pistols upset lots of grown-ups in England by making

Four blokes I'm glad I never shagged

their own version of 'God Save The Queen' which had rude words in it. All the silly old people who went mad and spluttered into their morning tea didn't realise that this meant the record would sell much better and make more money for Mr McClaren.

The boys in The Pistols decided to spread the word in America. They were very pleased with the results because there were lots of riots and this cheered them up almost as much as having a bottle of vodka or shagging a groupie. Sid Vicious retained his crown as the most admired member of the band by stabbing himself a lot.

The Sex Pistols were very pleased when a police officer said, 'I have never seen anything like this shower. They seem like a bunch of dangerous escaped lunatics. God knows what the kids see in them.'

Sid also admitted to smashing bottles and grinding them into his chest for that extra bit of teen admiration.

At a gig in America, Sid was head-butted by a teenage girl called Lamar. This made Sid's face bleed which in The Sex Pistols' book is very good thing. A roadie with the band, who

19

lived in the real world and didn't understand, wanted to smack Lamar back, but Sid stopped him and showed his appreciation by pulling a bandage covered in pus off his arm and throwing it to the crowd.

To make Sid's fairy-tale world complete, all he needed was a fairy-tale princess and she arrived in the form of Nancy Spungen whom Sid immediately fell in love with because she was a heroin addict and a go-go dancer.

Sid didn't want to buy his fairy-tale princess a little cottage with roses round the door; he wanted to earn enough money to pay for a birthmark to be removed from her bum so she could become a stripper. Nancy stayed in London while Sid was in America. But she wasn't wasting away dying of love for him; she was working as a prostitute to pay for her habit.

Wicked Malcolm McClaren tried to stop Sid going to New York to meet Nancy and have lots of heroin and poor Sid had to go in the bus round the southern states of America, doing gigs and cheering himself up by refusing to have a bath, cutting himself, passing out in his own vomit and consoling himself with other women, but showing he didn't really care by covering them with diarrhoea.

But our fairy-tale has a happy ending for Sid and Nancy. They were reunited in New York and Sid was so pleased to see Nancy he murdered her while they were both out of it.

He was given bail and then died of an overdose in the arms of his new girlfriend. And that, children, is the story of little Simon Beverly, the Prince of Punk.

An early Blue Peter sneering competition

20

MAHATMA
Gandhi

'It looked a lot better on Claudia Schiffer in Milan'

'No, not this photo for Dateline'

andhi was born in India, a member of a fairly high caste, which means that people who only washed on Tuesdays and Sundays were not allowed to touch him. He was no relation to Indira or Rajiv or Goosey Goosey. The only thing he had in common with them was assassination.

Poor old Gandhi had to get married at the age of 13 to another 13-year-old called Kasturbai. Gandhi decided as a child that he would be in charge of the marriage and so his wife had to ask him when she wanted to go out to play.

I don't agree with arranged marriages, but I suppose at least it means you can be sure of getting a husband...

Kasturbai got pregnant at 15 and around this time Gandhi's father became ill. While Gandhi took his turn to look after his father, he could not stop thinking about having sex with his

23

wife. Couldn't get it out of his mind. One night when his father was really ill, as his cousin arrived to take over, Gandhi rushed to have sex with his wife. A few minutes later a relative knocked on the door and by the time he got back to the sick room, his father was dead.

After that he always felt very guilty about sex. He didn't, however, worry that he had been demanding sex from his wife at other times which weren't very convenient for her; like when she wanted to go out skipping.

When he was a big boy, Gandhi went to London to train in law. In London he experimented with food and discovered that the real seat of taste was the mind not the tongue. I can't agree with that. I've never thought thinking about a big dinner was as good as actually shoving one down the old cakehole.

Gandhi started a neighbourhood vegetarian club, which was a bit like Neighbourhood Watch except you had to grass people up if you spotted them with a sausage.

From London he was sent to South Africa to fight a lawsuit and was shocked by the treatment of Asians there. South Africa has always been a civil rights nightmare. I've never bought South African fruit, in fact I've never bought any fruit at all.

One incident which stayed with Gandhi was when the police chucked him out of a first-class train compartment, even though he had a first-class ticket, just because he was Asian. He cites this as the time the seed of resistance was sown. I was thrown out of a first-class carriage once, but I didn't have a ticket, was smoking in a non-smoker and I was abusive to the guard. So that seemed pretty fair to me.

After the lawsuit was sorted, Gandhi prepared to return to

'Gandhi started a neighbourhood vegetarian club, which was a bit like Neighbourhood Watch except you had to grass people up if you spotted them with a sausage'

'Yeah, this one for Dateline'

India but was then asked to help fight against the bill to deprive Indians of voting rights. He said he'd stay on for a little while and ended up staying 20 years, which I suppose is a little while if you believe in reincarnation.

Gandhi had started to think about how unfair life was and when bubonic plague broke out, he volunteered to inspect toilets and included in his inspection the khazis of the untouchables and said their toilets were cleaner than the rich people's. This wound up the rich people as no one likes to be told they're dirty.

Gandhi supported Indians in resisting unfair laws. He was beaten up several times, but this seemed to strengthen his resolve, whereas one tap on the cheek is enough for me to slink back home and stop poking my nose in. Eventually Gandhi became recognised leader of the South African Asians.

Gandhi drove his poor old wife bonkers, interfering in household matters and making her carry out potties in the morning. Kasturbai thought she was above this but Gandhi pointed out that he was in charge and as soon as she'd finished he'd see her in bed.

From the age of 37, however, he took a vow of celibacy and his wife for once didn't object. It sounds like she had had enough sex to satisfy a rugby team on heat.

Gandhi was changing all the time. He tried really hard to become a nice person. He was even nice to horrible people. One of his close associates turned out to be an informer. Yet when this man became ill and poor, Gandhi visited him and gave him money.

Gandhi was provided with a farm by a kind rich person which was extremely fortunate because at the time there were only about three kind rich people in South Africa. On the farm Gandhi worried about the salacious looks that the young male workers on the farm gave the young females and persuaded all the girls to shave their heads so that boys wouldn't fancy them. I expect the boys were then scared of the girls because they thought they might burst into a chorus of 'Nothing Compares to U', or start slagging off the Pope.

Having sorted out some of the Asians' problems, Gandhi decided to move back to India where his prime target was Independence. He wanted the British out. And who can blame him? In those days every upper-class Englishman's life was broadly mapped out in advance: Eton, Oxford, the Guards, India, alcoholism and syphilis. Not any more, of course, thanks to penicillin.

Gandhi had a policy of non-violent co-operation with the British, who initially refused to negotiate with him until he renounced non-violence.

One weapon which Gandhi used very successfully was fasting. If ever anything went wrong he would fast until people gave in. I'd try this except no one would notice any difference for about six years.

'It's quite possible that the battle of Armageddon could begin with a conflict between teetotallers and vegetarians. So much for healthy living, eh?'

Gandhi also invented 'days of silence' when he would not talk to anyone. Lots of people thought this was for mystic religious reasons, but Gandhi said later he just fancied a day off and was fed up with people jabbering to him. He fought against specific issues like the British salt monopoly. Lots of Indians waded into the sea to collect salt and there were mass arrests. But at least their chips tasted better.

Eventually Gandhi had as much of a victory as he could and India won independence from Britain, although it had to be partitioned because of the Moslems.

In modern India it's as though Gandhi had never lived. Moslems and Hindus take to the streets with machetes at the drop of a turban and many people expect a full-scale war soon between Pakistan and India, both of whom possess nuclear weapons. Since Hindus don't eat meat and Moslems don't drink alcohol, it's quite possible that the battle of Armageddon could begin with a conflict between teetotallers and vegetarians. So much for healthy living, eh?

MR
Pankhurst

Having a three-legged dog sewn round the bottom of your coat was fashionable in Victorian times

Long-haired guinea pigs often lived in suffragettes hats

r Pankhurst was the new man of his generation. In Victorian times, men weren't known for their respect for women and children, and silly epigrams abounded like, 'children should be seen and not heard'. This is wrong, I think children shouldn't be seen or heard. And in those days many weren't because they were stuck up a chimney.

Mr Pankhurst somehow managed to swallow his pride and become a new man, years before male alternative comics were pretending they were. I asked a male friend of mine recently what a new man was and he said it was all about

31

learning how to cry and bonding. So I superglued his genitals to the bumper of my car and drove to Scotland. Loads of blubbering, loads of bonding, great.

Mr Pankhurst's wife and two daughters were the leading lights of the women's suffrage movement. In those days women didn't even have the vote and many of them weren't interested because they were too busy reading their horoscopes and discussing the latest eye-shadow. Thank God things have changed. They've got soap operas to watch as well now.

Mr Pankhurst could not understand why his missus chained herself to railings, then punched him in the goolies when he asked if he could tie her to the four-poster

When the Pankhursts made family decisions, Mr. P. was the only one who wasn't allowed to vote. If he put his hand up anyway, he was ignored. If they needed another opinion, they asked the dog.

All Mr Pankhurst knew was that quite often the house was full of women discussing committees and plans of action and so forth. Naturally he assumed it was to do with the local fête.

Mrs. Pankhurst's mob tried to get the vote for a long time by being nice and polite and going through the correct channels; women's suffrage bills were introduced and defeated in parlia-

'Imagine chaining yourself to some railings and then realising you'd left your fags in the car'

ment for over twenty years. This didn't work, though, because in a man's world you don't get anywhere by asking nicely. It's no good saying to lads on a stag night, 'Please don't abuse me in that way, I'm only a girlie.' Try 'Shut your mouths or I'll sit on your face' if you want to get anywhere. This is what the Pankhursts discovered. So they launched a militant campaign – smashing windows, cutting telephone wires and chaining themselves to railings!

I could never have done this. Imagine chaining yourself to

'Oi Panky, can't you control your Missus?'

some railings and then realising you'd left your fags in the car.

The suffragettes also set fire to pillar boxes, refused to pay taxes and bombed the home of the Chancellor of the Exchequer. All this and getting Mr Pankhurst's dinner every night, not to mention ironing his shirts and washing his underpants.

Mr Pankhurst kept his head down while this was going on because, every time he went to the pub, blokes would shout things like 'Oi Panky, can't you control your Missus?' or 'You must be under the thumb, mate.' Sometimes his wife would have to come down to the pub and sort them out.

Many suffragettes were imprisoned and force-fed when they went on hunger strike. Under the Cat and Mouse Act, they would be repeatedly released to regain their health, then re-arrested. This meant poor Mr. Pankhurst often had to eat in restaurants as there was no one at home to cook his meals. There is a version of the Cat and Mouse Act in operation

It was customary to hold up your spleen at a wedding

today except it is perfectly legal and is called 'going to a health farm'. Strangely enough women do this of their own volition.

Mr Pankhurst watched with horror as Emily Davidson threw herself under the king's horse in the 1913 Derby, then shook his head and tore up his ticket. He had never had any luck backing horses. Some guy recently threw himself in front of a

'He would sit at home weeping gently into the washing up. At least he had learned to cry without the help of some crass self-help book by an American psychologist who looks like Woody Allen'

horse at a race but this wasn't because of any burning desire to change unfair laws; it was because he was a student and he was pissed.

In the end Mr Pankhurst was so embarrassed by his wife that

34

he stopped seeing any of his male friends at all. He would sit at home weeping gently into the washing up. At least he had learned to cry without the help of some crass self-help book by an American psychologist who looks like Woody Allen

Eventually, of course, the suffragettes were successful. By degrees they won full suffrage. Unfortunately Mrs Pankhurst didn't live to see it and neither did Mr Pankhurst because this little piece has been a pack of lies. Mr Pankhurst actually died some time before the women in his family got going on the protest trail .Well, you've got to have something to fill your day if you haven't got a husband.

SIR WALTER *Raleigh*

Walter had a very sensitive hat that had learnt how to cry

*Walter's famous impersonation
of a Christmas tree*

alter Raleigh was born in 1552 and was the complete Elizabethan gentleman, soldier, courtier, poet, mariner, explorer and all-round ruff diamond.

He was born in Devon to a Protestant family and, despite going to Oxford and doing law, all he really wanted to do was go and have adventures. So he was a little boy at heart.

Raleigh was pronounced Rawley. He was quite pally (or should that be pawley?) with the Earl of Essex at first. They fell out over a woman of course.

At the age of 26 Little Wally was at sea destroying Spanish

shipping and two years later he fought against rebels in Ireland, gaining a reputation for ruthlessness. To gain a reputation for ruthlessness in Ireland at that time, you had to be a cross between Rupert Murdoch, Jeffrey Dahmer and Vlad the Impaler, because all the English in Ireland came under the heading of 'Your Common or Garden Psychopath'.

Historians think it is possible little Wally came to the notice of Elizabeth I because of his theories on quicker subjugation of Ireland. What a nice old bird she must have been. No

Queen Bess wonders if it's a gesture of kindness or a practical joke to chuck her arse over tit

crochet or madrigals for her, then. Oh no. It was 'Find me the biggest bastard in England and set him on the Irish'.

Raleigh became court favourite with Elizabeth I and it was he who spread his cloak on the ground for Elizabeth to step on. What a crawling little worm he was. He probably showered her with apples, carried her books home and put his hand up in class all the bleeding time. He was the child at school that you wanted to be taken away by the social services.

Elizabeth obviously fell for it because she knighted him and awarded him vast estates in Ireland. These were more trouble than they were worth – probably not enough people left to torture.

The highest position Little Wally achieved was Captain of

'Sadly poor old Queen Bess was never able to appreciate the full effect of fags. Never having hit the sack, she didn't have the chance to inhale the fag at its best... the après-shag shag'

the Queen's Guard. No one seems to know whether Little Walter ever romped Queen Bess. Considering she was called the Virgin Queen, it seems likely that they just indulged in a bit of heavy petting, leaving an intact hymen and a grumpy old lady.

One thing I have to get down on my knees and thank Little Wally for is his discovery of the heavenly substance, matchless in its supreme wonderfulness: tobacco. Oh, the gorgeousness of cigarettes. Sadly poor old Queen Bess was never able to appreciate the full effect of fags. Never having hit the sack, she didn't have the chance to inhale the fag at its best... the après-shag shag.

I would have suggested Little Wally's canonisation had it been true that he brought spuds over here as well. Potatoes, however, were not indigenous to Virginia, the bit of land he named after Bess, so people who love him for being potato man are wrong.

Raleigh's main rival for the Queen's affection was always the Earl of Essex. These two sad boys constantly vied with each other and, when one was in favour, the other was seriously in danger of losing his head.

In 1592 Queen Elizabeth discovered Raleigh's secret marriage to one of her maids of honour, Elizabeth Throckmorton. It's a bit unreasonable of a virgin queen to expect everyone else to be celibate. But she was the queen, so she could expect people to cut one leg off and hop round singing a selection of songs from Singalongamax if she wanted to. This is what fame and power does for you: it makes people around you behave like complete slavering drongos. This makes you feel far more important than you are, so that when they cross you, rather than stamping your foot and having a whinge, you

Walter's 'problem' meant he could only write standing up

go totally over the top and send them to the Tower of London.

So Little Wally and Throckers had their honeymoon in the Tower.

After he had done his porridge Little Wally embarked on his main career of exploration. He sailed up the Orinoco and discovered Guiana, which started the legend of the mythical city of Eldorado. Sadly in the 20th century lots of English people discovered Eldorado was a place where a load of really tedious characters who couldn't act lived, and tried to use it as an excuse not to pay their licence fee.

Little Wally joined his rival Essex in a major attack on Cadiz.

He was gradually replacing Essex in the affections of the Queen, so much so that in a rebellion in 1601, Essex and his followers attempted to murder him. Still Raleigh stayed calm and kept his head, which is more than Essex did.

When James I came to the throne in 1603, Raleigh was in trouble. James put him on trial for treason. He was convicted on the evidence of one of his close friends, Lord Cobham. Little Wally was reprieved from death at the last minute and confined in the Tower – almost like a second home to him, then. Still I suppose most people don't have whips and chains in their second homes – unless they're Tory MPs.

Wally was released in 1616 on the condition that he led an expedition to Guiana and returned with gold, without pro-voking the Spanish. But just as a British lad on holiday can't avoid throwing up everywhere and singing 'Roll Me Over' at the drop of a 'Kiss Me Quick' hat, so little Wally couldn't keep his sword to himself. He massacred loads of Spanish, the crews mutinied and he lost his ships. Foolishly he made the mistake of going back to England to tell the king about it and was beheaded. He said of the axe, 'Tis a sharp remedy but a sure one for all ills.' Good job he never tried stand-up comedy then.

'You sure there's only tobacco in this, 'cos this table's eating my finger!'

43

ELVIS
Presley

Elvis doing his famous impersonation of me

Elvis often worked part-time as a frying pan

Ivis Presley was born in 1935, the son of Gladys and Vernon. He had an identical twin Jesse who was stillborn. Just think what an effect the singing Presley twins might have had. They could have married two of The Nolans and ruled the world.

Elvis's dad, like all caring new men, was out on the piss when Elvis was born and throughout his childhood Elvis became very close to his mum and even slept in her bed at times. Some people have suggested they had an incestuous relationship. Well, I slept with my mum when I was a kid, but I never tried to get off with her.

As a teenager Elvis began playing in music clubs but the traditional country types took the piss out of him. This was probably because they all looked like extras from *Deliverance* and were jealous of his gorgeous sultry looks.

'It's much easier to send a note backstage asking if they fancy a quickie, then you don't have to expend any energy'

Gradually Elvis's career began to take off and at this point Colonel Tom Parker arrived on the scene to manage him. He was very bossy and protective of Elvis and even told him to stop seeing his girlfriend Pixie Locke as it created the wrong impression. Elvis agreed but always maintained Pixie was the only girl he'd ever loved. Blokes always tell you that they've only ever loved one girl, just so you won't start getting ideas about filling your bottom drawer and booking the church five minutes after you've met them.

Elvis was the first performer to drive girls wild. They would scream and cry and try to grab him. I've often wondered why they bother. It's much easier to send a note backstage asking if they fancy a quickie, then you don't have to expend any energy.

Soon Elvis was becoming incredibly rich and famous. He bought a big house and loads of cars for people as presents. He was so taken up with the fame bit for a while that he neglected his old mum who sat in Graceland all day drinking and feeling morose. When she died in 1957, Elvis felt very guilty and locked himself in his room for eight days.

Like all young American men, Elvis had to do National Service. Paying a million dollars in taxes wasn't enough. Fortunately for him Vietnam hadn't started yet, so he went to Germany and was put on singing duty. He was made welcome by the other troops, so he gave them all Cadillacs. On the parade ground an officer complimented him on his appearance, so Elvis gave him an aeroplane.

When Elvis joined the army, he gravitated towards young girls. I think this was because he thought he would not have to say much to them, because young girls tend to spend their time squealing a lot and reading *Smash Hits.*

Soon after returning from National Service, Elvis married Priscilla Beaulieu, the daughter of some army type in Germany. She was a tiny young thing, but with the 60s make-up you could look 40 when you were only 12 if you wanted to.

The Colonel wanted Elvis to marry Priscilla. Elvis didn't want to marry anyone but he did what he was told. When they did marry, Elvis was eyeing girls up in the lobby of the hotel, while Priscilla was probably thinking: 'Bloody hell, I've hooked the bastard. When can I start shopping?'

Elvis's behaviour was completely controlled by the Colonel. When Martin Luther King was assassinated, the Colonel wouldn't let Elvis talk publicly about it. This is because Col. Tom wanted Elvis's image to be that of sexy male bimbo and thought that, if Elvis got involved in controversy, he would sell fewer records. Let's not beat about the bush, Col. Tom was a money-grabbing, calculating little sod.

Poor old Elvis gradually became more and more lonely. He was moody and had odd eating and sleeping habits, which sadly for him he couldn't pass off as the menopause, because he wasn't old enough. He would gorge himself on junk food. (He

When Elvis was really hungry over 50 girls were needed to take his pizza order

and I could have had such a brilliant time together.)

He also sleepwalked, which worried Col. Parker. He didn't want to see his bread and butter go plummeting off a hotel balcony, so he employed guards to keep an eye on Elvis round the clock. The guard would wake him, soothe him and read him to sleep. What a sweet image, some great gorilla trying to make it all the way through *Goldilocks* without tripping over any words.

Because of his unhealthy lifestyle, Elvis had big boils on his bottom, but even today I bet we could find at least a million Elvis fans who would volunteer to lance them.

Elvis started to get more disturbed as time went on. At one point, he believed he could heal fans and control weather. His

Elvis often fell over backwards when he was a bit pissed

fans were so bonkers about him they believed it as well. Eventually Priscilla and Elvis separated, because celebrity marriages seem doomed to fail and every time Elvis said it would be a nice day for the beach, it rained.

A little known fact about Elvis is that Barbra Streisand wanted him to be in *A Star is Born* with her. The Colonel put the

'He would gorge himself on junk food. (He and I could have had such a brilliant time together)'

kibosh on this as well, because he didn't want Elvis portrayed as a junkie. This is a bit like Mike Tyson being asked to star in *Taxi Driver* and his manager turning it down because he doesn't want him portrayed as a thug.

The Russians called Elvis 'Public Enemy no. 1'. Possibly they had seen some of his films.

After Priscilla had left, Elvis had an affair with a woman called Linda Thompson who had won the dubious accolade of 'Best Dressed Student' at Memphis State University. Linda, sadly, was not Elvis's salvation; he was gradually getting the reputation of Worst Dressed Pop Star in The World, going out on stage looking like a cross between a Christmas tree and a Sumo wrestler.

He would sweat profusely, hair dye running down his face, and occasionally rip his trousers when he was performing. People were absolutely aghast at the condition he was in. Bloody hell, the guy was only fat for gawd's sake; he hadn't sexually abused children or strangled a lovely fluffy rabbit.

During this time Elvis was having lots of overdoses but no one close to him seemed to give a toss.

By 1976 he had glaucoma, an enlarged heart, hypoglycaemia, damaged kidneys, hypertension, a twisted colon and was seriously addicted to drugs. In fact he was a medical student's dream. His girlfriend Linda Thompson was getting on his nerves, so he got a private detective to chuck her out. Men have never been good at the more emotional side of communication.

Jo Brand – A Load of Old Balls

Elvis fell into a deep depression when some of the people closest to him cashed in with a kiss-and-tell book. It was downhill all the way from that point. In August 1977 he was found dead in the bathroom with his jamas round his ankles – a pretty undignified way to go, but I don't suppose Elvis was too worried about it.

I would say Elvis probably started off a pretty nice bloke, whose life was ruined by greedy people around him like Colonel Tom.

People were so crazy about Elvis they pretend he is still alive. Apparently he's always in Tescos and what good taste . . . they have lovely cakes there.

'She's how old!?'

52

Kim *Philby*

The back of Kim Philby's head was very boring indeed

Kim trying to pretend he isn't a spy

hen I was a kid, I always wanted to be a spy. This was because it seemed to me that all you had to do was sit on a park bench and occasionally poke someone with a poisoned umbrella. I also thought that it would give me a chance to track down James Bond and finish the macho oversexed creep off once and for all, not to mention all those silly women he hangs around with like Pussy Galore. (James dear, I for one would definitely shut my cat flap if you knocked on my door.)

Kim Philby was one of those spies who committed the most heinous of crimes (apart from forgetting the phone number for

Pizza Express) he was a double agent, working for the Russians and the Brits. People hate him because he sent innocent people to their deaths. Of course politicians do this as well, but only for jolly good reasons, like protecting some oil or a few sheep in the Atlantic.

'A socialist society has to work as hard to survive at Cambridge as Peter Stringfellow at a Roly-Polies' convention'

Philby was born in India in 1911 and had what you would call a posh boy's upbringing. He went to Westminster School and on to Cambridge at the age of 17. You may be wondering at this point why such a privileged little boy with everything going for him decided to work for the downfall of his government, rather than doing what all the others do, which is swan about round gentlemen's clubs talking drivel and working at the BBC.

Well, it all seems to hang on the fact that at Cambridge he joined a Socialist society.

A Socialist society has to work as hard to survive at Cambridge as Peter Stringfellow at a Roly-Polies' convention, so those who joined were obviously very committed.

The rout of the Labour party in 1931 completely pissed off young Kim. He couldn't understand how 'a supposedly sophisticated electorate had been stampeded by the cynical propaganda of the day'. Perhaps he was a bit naïve. I find it very easy to believe.

After Cambridge, Kim went to Vienna and became a Soviet agent. Funnily enough he doesn't mention this in his autobiography, so we have to imagine exactly what happened. I expect a mysterious-looking man in a trilby said to him in broken English, 'The geese fly south in winter', then they had a vodka and agreed Stalin was a good bloke. (Well, I have watched *The Spy Who Came In From The Cold*, you know.)

Kim took a trip to Spain during the Civil War. Many people in

Spain think the Civil War is still going on, due to the fact that their homes are near resorts where English people go on holiday.

In1940 Philby joined MI5 which was very easy to get into, so easy in fact that at one point his secret Russian contact thought he must have joined a different organisation. If only he had and if only it had been the Women's Institute, he might at this very moment be sitting in a house in Surrey having coffee, trying to flog padded coat-hangers and attempting to arm the Neighbourhood Watch. Considering Kim was recruited into the secret service by a lady called Marjorie, I think it's very possible he was in the WI.

Kim was nearly rumbled a few times. He describes one incident in Spain when he was arrested and had some code instructions in his trousers and no chance to dispose of them. When he was in the interview room, he threw his wallet to the end of the table and all the policemen made a grab for it while he swallowed the code. Reassuring to know the police are as daft as brushes the world over. Rumour has it they bought some double glazing off him after that.

At one time Kim became convinced that German Intelligence were trying to recruit him. He was wined and dined by a German intelligence officer who in fact just wanted to get off with a woman Kim knew. And there's me thinking spies were dedicated, brave, hard-bitten men who were obsessed with high-faluting moral questions – ruled by their todgers like every other man on the planet.

'he might at this very moment be sitting in a house in Surrey having coffee, trying to flog padded coat-hangers and attempting to arm the Neighbourhood Watch'

Kim's boss was Guy Burgess and his department never had enough money to carry out ideas – a bit like the NHS really. He started a training school for agents but the Commander had very bad eczema and resigned, so the whole thing fell apart.

This isn't really painting a picture of what's called 'intelligence' is it?

'Kim was given a luxurious one-room apartment in Moscow with cardboard walls and all the candles he could eat. So it was well worth it then'

They sound like a right bunch of no-hopers to me. Still they were blessed with razor-sharp interrogation techniques as the following story illustrates.

A woman who had entered England from Portugal and was known to consort with German intelligence officers was taken in for interrogation. She had with her a little diary with cryptic abbreviations. When questioned by British intelligence, she denied any German acquaintance and after hours of interrogation still would not crack and spill the beans. Eventually the man questioning her made one last attempt. There was an entry in her diary which said, 'spent all day sitting on my fanny'. The interrogator seized upon this and asked, 'Who is Fanny? Why were you sitting on her?'

According to Kim Philby, under such bizarre, yet clever questioning, the woman broke down and confessed all. Well, I've had enough of this. That is the biggest load of old rubbish I have ever heard in my entire life and if this is an example of the skills of British intelligence, I think we can forget it.

You probably know the rest anyway. Kim went to America, his mates Burgess and Maclean hopped it to Russia and then he decided he'd better go too.

He buried his spying gear in the woods and met a Russian. 'What passed there,' he says in his biography, 'is no concern of the reader.' Or interest either, Kim. I expect Kim became a solid Soviet citizen, with all the privileges that implies, and was given a luxurious one-room apartment in Moscow with cardboard walls and all the candles he could eat. So it was well worth it then.

58

J Ed pretending to be nice

Edgar was like a sewer who collected dirt.'
Well, that quote kicks us off in the right direction, I think. J Edgar could never have worked for the AA; by
no stretch of the imagination could he have been described as
'a very, very nice man'.

He was born at the end of the 19th century and as a child
he was highly strung, excessively fearful and very boring. His
diary at the age of 13 contains such fascinating details as the
extent of cloud cover and the temperature. It also lists his hat
and collar sizes. The man, according to Freud's theories, seems
to have been stuck at the anal stage of development. In other
words, he was a bit of an arsehole. His nickname at college

61

was fatty pants, I suppose because his pants were fat.

When he grew up, Hoover's main facial feature was a squashed-looking nose. J Ed said this was because of a sporting accident, but his niece spoilt this by saying it was the result of a boil that had healed badly.

'it sounds like something Goebbels dashed off before he put in an order for some more piano wire'

Old Boil Nose never had any girlfriends. Not surprising really. He didn't like any women except his mum, which always seems to be a recipe for future badness. He was against the vote for women. He didn't want his mum reading the political pages of the *Independent* when she should have been getting his dinner on the table.

J Ed's fave bit of poetry is very revealing about his attitude to society:

Only the strong shall thrive,
That surely the weak shall perish and
only the fit survive

First of all it's crap poetry and secondly it sounds like something Goebbels dashed off before he put in an order for some more piano wire.

Hoover is famous for being the head of the FBI, which was established to deal with crimes that crossed state borders. Before it was set up you could slaughter your family in one state and nip to the one next door to get another one.

J Ed's attitude towards the fair sex wasn't improved when he was let down by a woman called Alice who two-timed him with a soldier. She was obviously a glutton for punishment: 'Mmm. Shall I go out with an obsessive mummy's boy or someone who likes shooting people?' Neither, Alice dear, would be the sensible advice.

Even when he was a grown-up, J Ed behaved like Spoilt Brat from *Viz*. If his breakfast egg was broken, he wouldn't eat it.

𝒥 Edgar Hoover

J Ed about to put his strongest glasses on to examine his breakfast egg

Why did his mum put up with this tyrannical behaviour? Probably because he was her blue-eyed squashed-nose boy and she said to herself: 'One day he's going to be head of the FBI and treat thousands of people like shit, just like he does me.'

J Ed gradually worked his way up the FBI, starting with small-time stuff like brutal attacks on the Union of Russian Workers, and ended up becoming a mason.

Because he didn't have a girlfriend he kept a picture of his dog on desk at work.

BY 1924 Hoover was head of the FBI. His agents nicknamed him Kid Napoleon but he didn't have a Josephine and in a sulky way tried to prevent his agents from marrying.

He was completely obsessive about tidiness and once had a go at an official who had a window blind pulled down, because it made the building look untidy. I'm surprised no one realised he was barking at that point and had him locked up.

Hoover was also opposed to hiring black people and

J Ed and JFK compare notches on their bedsteads

women. When he started as head there were three women in the department. He had two sacked and the third went mad and was sent to a mental hospital, where she threatened to shoot him as soon as she was released. J Ed said women could never gunfight, but he didn't take the risk with this agent just in case. He would not allow women to smoke or wear pants to work – pants, in the American sense, that is. J Ed was a well-known perv but that didn't start until later.

J Ed's prevailing attitude to women, according to someone who knew him, was: 'Bullshit 'em and ball 'em; don't tell 'em any secrets.' He must have got this bit of advice out of *The World Manual Of How Blokes Should Treat Women* by several of my ex-boyfriends.

He also believed that, when a woman turns criminal, she is a hundred times more vicious, and had a strange idea that female criminals always had red hair or wore a red wig. How his agents kept a straight face I do not know.

Hoover's 'life-long companion' (which was a euphemism in

those days for gay lover) was Clyde Tolson. He and Clyde were apparently spotted together in public holding hands on a number of occasions. I have no objection to that but J Ed did go round slagging off gays and pretended to have women friends to throw people off the scent and borrow their clothes for the odd orgy. The orgies were odd because J Ed would appear looking like Arthur Mullard in drag.

Schoolboys voted him second most popular man in America, which just goes to show how unreliable a school-boy's opinion is on anything.

Of course J Ed is most famous for his role in the McCarthy witch-hunts against suspected Communists. Walt Disney actually

'The orgies were odd because J Ed would appear looking like Arthur Mullard in drag'

testified in court that several conspirators at the Disney studios were attempting to use Mickey Mouse to spread Communist propaganda. And that sums up what a complete farce the whole episode was.

One of J Edgar's biggest hates was Eleanor Roosevelt, the President's wife. He said he never married because God made women like Eleanor Roosevelt. The reason he hated her was because she was a decent, caring person who campaigned for better housing and fair treatment of black people.

J Ed liked to have a giggle at three miniature portraits of Eleanor which, upside down were grotesque anatomical views of a woman's vagina. Thankfully this utterly revolting creature did eventually die. If I ever go to America I must brush up my dancing skills, so I can have a little jig on his grave.

LORD
Byron

'No dear, it's about six inches bigger than that'

*Byron wowed the House of Lords with his
Steve Davis impression*

yron was a great source of distress to me as a teenager because someone I was madly in love with chucked me with a bit of his poetry entitled 'We'll go no more a roving'. Unfortunately for my ex, Byron hadn't written a poem called 'I'm going out with someone else now and you're boring'.

In theory he could have done, though, because Byron was your archetypal ladies' man. He didn't so much sow his wild oats as lob great handfuls of them to all the corners of the universe.

He wasn't much of a romantic hero to look at, having a club

foot and a bit of a dumpy frame, but he certainly had something, because he had women queueing up to be chewed and spat out.

'he was posh and he was a poet, so women would have given him one even if he'd looked like Freddie Kruger'

Plusses in the scoring market for Byron were that he was educated at Cambridge, so he could talk proper; he was a Lord, so he was posh; and he was a poet, so women would have given him one even if he'd looked like Freddie Kruger.

He inherited the family title from a great-uncle and therefore had a seat in the House of Lords which he sat in a few times but didn't make a career of. Obviously there were more exciting things to do, like staring at a wall.

Byron's first published work was called 'Hours of Idleness' and by all accounts wasn't much cop. It got a scathing review in an Edinburgh magazine to which Byron responded, not in a mature and measured way but with a long and childishly petulant piece titled 'English Bards and Scotch Reviewers'.

I like this. I hate getting bad reviews, even if they're well deserved, and any comic who has done the Edinburgh Festival will know the blind rage that reviewers can engender. Some papers are so busy at Edinburgh Festival time that they have to use people like the gardening correspondent to do reviews. I once got a review in Edinburgh about a show I was in which said, 'Jo Brand is fat.' And that was it – not from a minimalist dieting magazine as you might imagine, but just some sulky student whom I'd liked to have sat on.

When Byron got bored with the House of Lords he went on a tour of the Mediterranean with a mate. This was a bit like an extended 18-30 holiday except they had about twelve thousand more words in their vocabulary.

When Byron returned to England he published the first two parts of 'Childe Harold's Pilgrimage'. This is what made him

Byron's wife doing an impersonation of me

famous and before he could say, 'Anyone want to see my etchings,' ten cohorts of women were standing at his bedroom door.

Perhaps his most famous affair was with Lady Caroline Lamb, a married woman who did her best to play Liz Taylor to his Richard Burton. They went at it hammer and tongs and at one point Lady Caroline was moved to send Byron some pubic hair she had pulled out, still covered in blood. I wonder if that had to go registered post and what she wrote in the 'description of contents' section. Besides, I'm sure Byron would have pre-

71

ferred a nice postcard of Horse Guards Parade.

Byron is also said to have had an affair with his half-sister Augusta. Obviously his chances of becoming Poet Laureate were becoming slimmer by the minute.

But Byron did make an attempt at a normal marriage, so people would stop saying he was 'mad, bad and dangerous to be in the pub with'. He married a woman called Anne Milbanke who is described as priggish and self-righteous. On his wedding night he sat up and said, 'I am in hell.' Poor old Anne must have wondered whether she'd practised love bites enough on her pillow.

'Judging by the notches on his bed, he must be the best disguised homosexual until Jason Donovan'

Some people have proffered the theory that Byron had homosexual tendencies. Judging by the notches on his bed, he must be the best disguised homosexual until Jason Donovan (yeah I know about the court case, I'm only trying to make a point).

Byron got Anne pregnant and they separated after the birth. He left England, never to return. Perhaps he had heard rumours about the Child Support Agency.

He went to Switzerland and lived with Shelley and Mrs Shelley on the edge of Lake Geneva for a while. Mary Shelley wrote Frankenstein which was about a monster created by man, so she could just have easily called it Multi-Storey Car Park.

Byron was keeping up the nomping quotient. He was followed around by someone called Clair Claremont, but as we women know, if you nail your colours to the mast, the bloke tends to dump on you. She did and he did.

Byron then buggered off to Italy for six years and got into politics and someone called Theresa Guiccioli. He was as madly in love with her as a bloke like him could be, which

72

meant that if something more exciting came up, he would go off and do that instead. It did. Byron, who always had more of a social conscience and lefty leanings than the other lords of the day, decided to go and help the Greeks fight for their independence.

He fitted out a boat and sailed for Greece. He got as far as Missalonghi but before he'd had a chance to get involved in the fighting, he became ill and died. Still it seems appropriate that he died not on the battlefield, but where his greatest adventures had taken place...in the sack. By the way his poems are quite good too.

BENITO Mussolini

The Duce gestures his displeasure at yet another nippy Fiat cutting him up at the lights

'Unless the boy who stole my other glove comes forward, the whole of Italy will stay behind for detention'

enito Mussolini was born in 1883 near Forli in Romagna, in north-eastern Italy. His father was a bit of a rebellious type, a Socialist and a blacksmith.

Mussolini had a rather undistinguished educational career marred by several unpleasant acts of violence. This is the perfect combination of events for only one job... that's right, he became a schoolmaster. Having had some very unpleasant experiences as a child with teachers who were in the running, personality-wise, for jobs as Fascist dictators, it's not hard to see the comparison. Many teachers I knew had developed the ability to humiliate, intimidate and emotionally to destroy children, and had they been in charge of a country, they might well have gone down the same path as good old Benito.

As well as being a teacher, Benito was also a casual labourer for a while, and did military service. All my worst nightmare men gathered together in one. He was also involved with a Socialist newspaper. So was Robert Maxwell but that didn't prevent him behaving like the Antichrist.

Mussolini was expelled from the paper because he supported intervention in the First World War. He'd seen what a good spanking could do. He didn't think the Italians were capable of revolution but was interested in the power of nationalism as a popular force. The BNP are interested in the power of nationalism as a popular force as well, but fortunately only a couple of them can actually manage to say the whole sentence and the rest have to be content with squeezing out the odd grunt.

In 1919 Mussolini was responsible for setting up the Fascio di Combattimento with roughly a hundred other people including war veterans and dissident Leftists: the word 'fascio' came from the Latin word for the rods carried by magistrates of the Roman republic. Lots of silly words come from the Romans. The word 'testify' comes from testicles because when Roman men were in court swearing an oath they had to clutch their testicles. It does work, actually. If you clutch a bloke's testicles quite hard, he swears an oath. He really does, I know.

The new Fascist movement was supposed to be a challenge for left-wing working-class support and they were keen on the suffrage of women. Makes a change as most cultures up to this point were keen on the suffering of women.

The Fascists did not get many votes in the election, but then rich blokes got interested who could see the party's anti-Socialist potential. It's always bloody rich blokes, isn't it, looking for another way of making a buck.

To put the icing on the cake 'squadrismo' were set up. These were groups of thugs fighting against Socialism and trade unions. Today they are called followers of Thatcherism. They attacked offices of left-wing parties and Catholic peasant leagues. They used clubs, knives, guns and, on occasion, the forced consumption of castor oil. So people were in a right state, but at least their bowels were regular. The police authorities let the squadrismo get on with it – well, I suppose it meant they didn't have to expend all their energy going round beating people up themselves. The squadrismo managed to destroy the structure of rural Catholic and Socialist trade unionism in northern Italy. What clever boys. I bet 'Sir' gave them a gold star and let them off being milk monitor for a whole week.

These 'fasci' proliferated and the bigger organisations were headed by 'ras', bosses, a word from the Ethiopian for chieftain. Didn't anyone at this point think what a complete bunch of pathetic little children these people were? That's the problem; I'm sure they did, in the way I think that about Millwall hooligans. Problem is they're bigger than me and they can just give me a good kicking.

In 1921 the Fascists became a grown-up political party, the Partito Nazionale Fascista, and within a year Mussolini was

'They used clubs, knives, guns and, on occasion, the forced consumption of castor oil. So people were in a right state, but at least their bowels were regular'

79

headmaster – I mean Prime Minister. Mussolini became Prime Minister by refusing to join any government he did not lead. For two years he presided over a coalition government. The violence continued. The ras changed their name to consuls, in the same way that Derek Beackon changed his to councillor, and they all demanded Mussolini became a dictator. Well, this was the opportunity he'd been waiting for. Political opposition and free TV were banned, the free press was censored and taken over, elected local governments were replaced by appointed officials (today we call these quangos) and a police state was created. The scope of the death penalty was widened and special courts for political crimes were set up. And, of course, to control all this they needed a secret police, which was called OVRA. They made sure people did their homework, wore their school caps and didn't write graffiti in the toilets.

Mussolini was vain, capricious and authoritarian and those are about the only positive things you can say about him. He was jealous of France and Britain and wanted an empire all of his own, so in 1935 he started a war in Ethiopia and got a slice of land. I bet the poor old ras were pissed off. Mussolini had nicked their names and now he'd nicked their country as well.

Mussolini was renamed round about this point and his new name was Il Duce, 'the leader'. I don't know whether they had a national competition to find a name for him, as they did with the *Blue Peter* dog,

but I suppose not. I expect he thought 'Shep' would have made him look silly. He looked silly enough as it was: Humpty Dumpty in an army uniform.

Headmaster Mussolini then looked around for some rucks to get involved in, but secretly I don't think his army had much respect for him, because they were always getting trounced. He made his son-in-law Minister of Defence, obviously so if he didn't do what he was told, Mussolini could just ring up his daughter and tell her to have a headache.

During the Second World War the Italians, it has to be said, weren't much cop. They made minuscule advances into France, their attempt at invading Greece was crap, they lost their African empire, they stupidly declared war on the US and they supported Hitler. They couldn't have done worse if they'd had Eddie the Eagle leading the country. It was really only a matter of time before they got stuffed.

Things were going badly for Il Duce. He was sick with gastric trouble, although many people now believe this was psychosomatic. (Are Fascists intelligent enough to have psychosomatic disorders? I doubt it.) By this point Mussolini had surrounded himself with toadies. Perhaps he meant to dissect them in double biology. He went to meet Hitler but was too scared to tell him he didn't want to fight any more. That's the thing with bullies who teach. Put them up against someone's dad who is a bigger bully and they're in trouble.

Italians had had enough of Mussolini by now. They'd started to hear all those jokes like: 'What's the shortest book in the world? The book of Italian war heroes.' Mussolini was arrested, and now that he was in prison all the Italians he had forced to wear plimsolls for running away could take them off. Fascism collapsed and civil war started. Mussolini was rescued by the Germans and installed as the head of a new Fascist regime in the north of Italy. That lasted about as long as a Chippendale on a hen night. The Allies invaded. Mussolini was captured by the resistance and shot. His body was hung upside-down in a petrol station in Milan, so people could see he wasn't lead free.

GERONIMO

*Experts at tracking the Bison of the Great Plains,
the Apaches were nevertheless crap at hunting Water Buffalo*

To finance his guerrilla war, Geronimo secured lucrative sponsorship deals from the Hat Shop and Tie Rack

've often wondered what Geronimo shouted when he jumped over a cliff. Must have been 'Me!'

Geronimo was a Chiricahua Apache, whose motto was, 'There is food everywhere if you only know how to find it!' Similar to mine which is, 'There is food. Find it!'

The Apaches most prized food was mescal cactus, which they roasted and sun-dried. This was like LSD except it was less easily lost down the back of the settee.

In battle the Apaches were famous for cunning rather than

recklessness. Their numbers were so few that they had to fight by guerrilla tactics. This involved popping out from behind a cactus, totally out of their heads, and firing an aubergine at the cavalry. Well, they were stoned a lot.

They knew where every water hole in their terrain was and could wear out any pursuers by thirst. This is similar to blokes who know where every pub in their area is and can wear out their pursuers by talking about where every pub in their area is. The Apache technique for overcoming thirst was simply to put a pebble in their mouths. They were still thirsty but at least they couldn't talk about it.

Everybody had had a pop at the Apaches and they were getting sick of it. First it was the Spanish, then the Mexicans. The Spanish had supplied them with guns, horses and playing cards, so they'd have a quick round of Beat Your Neighbour Out Of Doors by jumping on their horses, taking their guns and shooting some Mexicans. Then they'd come back and play poker.

'The Apache technique for overcoming thirst was simply to put a pebble in their mouths. They were still thirsty but at least they couldn't talk about it'

Geronimo was born around 1829. His original name, Goyakhia, meant Yawner. His grandfather was a chief who got on with the Mexicans and lived peacefully. He achieved this by shelling out loads of dosh and saying the Mexicans were nice blokes.

When Geronimo was a teenager his father died. He was buried in a cave, his horse was shot and his name was never spoken again. Bit of an odd custom, not being able to mention the horse's name again.

Geronimo then headed off with his mum and joined the warlike Nednhi. I don't think his mum had much of a say in it but I'm sure she'd have preferred to stay with the happy peaceful people.

Geronimo

The Nednhi hated the Mexicans. There was constant trouble because the Mexicans wanted to mine copper on Indian land. Rather than having a cosy chat about this the Mexicans offered money for scalps. Lots of people think the Indians started the scalping business but in fact it was the civilising settlers who taught these savages just what being part of polite society meant.

By now Geronimo was a trained warrior. He married a Nednhi called Alope, which means, 'attracted to yawning', and had three kids. His wife, mother and kids were slaughtered with many other families by the Mexican army, outside a small town where the Nednhi were trading. Geronimo vowed to avenge them and with two other chiefs fought the Mexicans at a town called Arispe. Unsurprisingly Geronimo went berserk and charged at the Mexicans time and time again. Each time he charged, they called out to their patron saint Jerome, which in Spanish is Geronimo. Yes, I think you can guess what's coming. That's how. . . Oh, forget it.

Geronimo got two new wives (probably thinking there was safety in numbers), one of whom was quickly murdered by the Mexicans. Well, I don't suppose anyone at this point would be advising Geronimo to have a nice cup of tea with the other side and make it up. He became an even more obsessed Mexican-hater and even had some enemies in his own tribe who thought he was a nutter. Apparently they wanted him to change his name to Vinny Jones.

Aound this time Geronimo had a vision in which he was told he would never be killed by a bullet. Not particularly reassuring as those civilised white folk had lots of other unappetising ways of bumping off the Indians.

Following on from the Mexicans it was now the turn of the Americans to make everyone's life a misery. A chief, Cochise,

'The Apaches, very wisely, legged it but were rounded up and taken in chains to "Hell's forty acres", now known as Disneyland'

was wrongly accused of abducting a boy, and his brother and two nephews were hung in reprisal. Cochise, Geronimo and another chief Mangas Coloradas joined forces and it looked as if there would be civil war. Mangas Coloradas decided to make peace and went to the mining town of Pinos Altos to arrange a settlement. He was tortured, shot and decapitated and had his head boiled to be sent east as a phrenology exhibit. Scalping? Head boiling? No wonder Americans love Hannibal Lecter.

The Indians again launched a series of maniacal attacks but eventually Cochise and Mangas Coloradas's successor Victorio made peace. Geronimo wasn't having any of this and went off on his own engaging in the odd raid from time to time. He thought Victorio and Cochise were big girls' blouses.

Then the Americans had one of their worst ideas ever (apart from Dr Ruth). They invented reservations, making it worse by thinking they were doing the Indians a favour. The Apaches, very wisely, legged it but were rounded up and taken in chains to 'Hell's forty acres', now known as Disneyland. Geronimo stuck it out for two years. He then spent the next few years buggering off from the reservation for the occasional rumble. Think of these as Leeds United away games.

At one point rules were laid down on the reservation about beer drinking and putting a stop to the Indian custom of cutting off the tip of a married woman's nose if she was unfaithful. Oh dear, and just when I was starting to feel a bit of sympathy for the Apaches as well. I can't imagine any of Geronimo's wives daring to be unfaithful to him. He wasn't the most calm of men when things went wrong and he'd cut off far more important things than the tips of people's noses.

Geronimo became quite famous in later years. There were lots of articles in newspapers about him and he eventually moved to Oklahoma and sold souvenirs. Hopefully the tips of wives' noses stall didn't do very well.

I'd always assumed Geronimo died gloriously in battle but in fact he got pissed, fell off his horse, slept in damp weeds and contracted pneumonia. That's why I shout 'Geronimo' when I can feel a bit of a cold coming on.

BOB
Dylan

'All I said to Hendrix was "My version of 'All Along the Watchtower' is better than yours," and he poked me here with a biro'

*'I've heard Hendrix is in town and I'm taking
no chances'*

an Bob Dylan sing? This is a question which many people have answered 'no' to. It is true that he is very easy to do an impression of: you just growl in an American accent and sound like you've had a handful of hallucinogenics. But millions of old hippies all round the world love Bob and know everything he ever wrote, word for word. And his lyrics, although they are fairly inaccessible at times, do make for slightly more pleasant listening than Snoop Doggy Dogg railing against women in the style of Peter Sutcliffe.

Bob Dylan was born Robert Zimmerman in Minnesota and seems to have had a very ordinary youth until he discovered music. He then made the metamorphosis from a rather unattractive hairy youth to a rather unattractive hairy youth who was so famous everyone wanted to sleep with him. He seems to have been the sort of bloke that women wanted to mother.

'When I was 15, it was a strict requirement that my parents and friends hated someone or I wouldn't go out with them'

It's strange, this mothering syndrome that's been instilled into us girls: much as you kick against it, sometimes you just can't help pulling someone's shirt off and washing it.

The first girl our Bob was serious about was called Judy Rubin. She said, 'My parents didn't like him, neither did my friends, and that separated us.' Strange woman. When I was 15, it was a strict requirement that my parents and friends hated someone or I wouldn't go out with them. So, after Judy chucked Bob, he moved on to Bonnie Beecher. She got involved with him on the way to her finals, when she saw him lying in the middle of the road covered in vomit. She picked him up and cleaned him up. Well I suppose you'd want to have him vomit-free before you gave him one. In fact she was kicked out of college for associating with him. She stole food for him. Silly cow. If you're going to steal food, steal it for yourself.

'Well I suppose you'd want to have him vomit-free before you gave him one'

Once Bob realised that, vomit or not, he could get women in the sack, he went for it in a big way. He described one incident when he was 19 and a 'really old' woman picked him up. When a 19-year-old boy says he was picked up by a really old woman, he means a 25 or 26-year-old. Bob, however says this woman was at least 60 years old and had filed down her teeth. This probably means she was in her early 30s.

Bob also had quite a liking for drink and drugs and friends say that, when he was completely out of his head, he could still pick up a guitar and play. How irritating. The only bit of peace I

Hey chicks! I can always put a bag on my head

used to get from early angst-ridden boyfriends playing something by Joy Division was when they were too pissed to pick up their guitar. An article I read about Bob said he had a penchant for plump big-breasted women. Oh, for God's sake, what bloke doesn't? Men might appear in public with a lolly stick on two toothpicks but secretly, as so many blokes tell me when they're putting the bag over my head to take me down the pub, 'I like something to hold on to.'

Dylan's first proper girlfriend was called Suze Rotolo and he indulged in a game of double standards with her, sleeping around and going mad with her if she did. Suze apparently 'freaked out'. This is a quaint 70s term covering a variety of behaviour from silly hippy dancing to mad rage, and I don't think Suze did silly hippy dancing. Bob also had a relationship with Joan Baez, whom you won't have heard of unless you're over 35. Joan, unfortunately, was madly in love with Bob and this is the equivalent for some men of having a sign on your head saying 'Torture me until I lose my mind'. Poor old Joan eventually got the message when she turned up at Bob's room to see how he was after a bout of food poisoning and found a 'chick' in his room. This is a quaint 70s term for woman, which is supposed to be nicer than saying 'bird'. But it isn't. One woman did actually manage to get old Bob up to the altar. 'Mysterious American beauty' (how many mysterious Americans do you know?) Sara Lowndes played the right games and led Bob up the aisle. Happily ever after? We'll see.

95

Jo Brand – A Load of Old Balls

One problem Bob Dylan had that I can quite easily identify with was his relationship with the press. He reputedly 'mishandled' the press, which means he made the mistake of saying anything at all to them. The press picked up on his support for civil rights and had a good old bash at crucifying him. Following a slanging match with a *Newsweek* reporter, the said reporter implied in an article that someone else had written 'Blowing in the Wind'. I would have thought he'd have been glad to get that old chestnut pinned on someone else; and by the way, does anyone actually know how many seas a white dove has to sail before she sleeps in the sand?

One thing Bob Dylan used to do was to play 'mindgames' with people. This is a quaint 70s term meaning that he tried to wind people up for no reason. Whether this was because fame had affected him or he was just a prat has never been established. Unfortunately Bob started playing mindgames with entire nations. On tour he wound the French up and also got to the point at the Albert Hall where he was forced to say to a punter, 'Come up here and say that.' Luckily for him, whoever it was didn't.

Dylan's life changed after he had a motorbike accident. He is supposed to have 'lost it' the day he fell off his bike. People now say they don't believe he had an accident at all. I'm sure they could just phone the local garage and check. He tried to beat up a journalist who had been hanging round his house and looking in his dustbin for evidence of drugs, so he hadn't lost it completely. But his marriage broke up and he didn't talk to anyone for two days after Elvis Presley died, so maybe he was losing it a bit … and then he had a born-again experience in a hotel room, a vision of Christ. Oh blimey! He enrolled at

The Vineyard School of Discipleship. He said they were hypocritical but began preaching a bit at his gigs anyway.

The general theory about Bob Dylan seems to be that he wants to immunise himself against the power of women because he has realised they are not his salvation. Poor old bastard. All that success, all that money, and still not happy. My friend Kristina's looking for a bloke. I might try and get his number for her.

'Here Bob, Jimi just choked on his own vomit; you can take the shades off now'

97

MARGARET *Thatcher*

Mrs T with a pair of wets' testicles as earrings

'We are a robot'

am including Margaret Thatcher in this learned tome as an honorary man. I know she's not a man but I still think she should be strung up by the bollocks.

Margaret was born in Grantham. Her father was Alfred Roberts who owned a couple of grocers' shops and became Mayor of Grantham.

Margaret was hard-working at school but not brilliant. Apparently her family were strict and puritanical and she spent her life trying to escape. She still ended up exactly like them, though. At Oxford, while studying chemistry, she discovered

Conservatism. (I expect she inhaled something nasty.) Although she joined the Conservative Association, she couldn't join in any of the debates because women weren't allowed in. That never seemed to worry Margaret though. She is quoted, on feminism, as saying,'What's it ever done for me?' Well, only got you the vote, Missus.

I did a debate on feminism recently at Oxford and was very impressed by the sophisticated argument of the other team, which involved accusing me of having hairy armpits, being fat and not washing my hair often enough. It's comforting to know the future leaders of this country are so on the ball, isn't it?

'In 1975 Margaret became the leader of the Conservatives and began employing an image maker, who instructed the hairdresser to backcomb her hair up a bit more to hide the horns'

After leaving Oxford Margaret had two jobs in three years. She worked at a plastics firm and then got a job at J Lyons testing the quality of ice cream and cake fillings. Now I really do hate her. I went for that job and didn't get it. In 1949 Margaret met the lovely Denis Thatcher. He was a cut above her socially and had a glamorous job running a company producing weedkiller and sheep dip. Pity she didn't have to test those...

Not content with bossing her husband about, however, Maggie decided her country needed her and went into politics. She became MP for Finchley and worked in pensions for a while. Poor pensioners.

When the Tories won the election, she became Secretary of State for Education and Science. Quickly developing her technique of going for the innocent and defenceless, she cut children's free milk in primary schools. (I had always assumed it was she who instructed the teacher to put the milk on the radiators during the winter so it was warm and revolting.) This

'Just do what I do, Denis'

inspired piece of caring politics gained her the nickname Thatcher the Milk Snatcher and she got a lot of stick for it. Denis tried to persuade her to get out of politics. But she did not listen to him any more than she did to the rest of the universe.

In 1975 Margaret became the leader of the Conservatives and began employing an image maker, who instructed the hairdresser to backcomb her hair up a bit more to hide the horns. The image man was called Gordon Reece and he had the privilege of hearing one of the few Thatcher jokes. She said to him, 'If we lose the election, I may be sacked but you will be shot.' Gordon, I don't think that was a joke, mate.

Mrs T became Prime Minister in 1979. When she arrived at Downing Street, she quoted Francis of Assisi's famous passage, where he promises to double unemployment and abolish the Welfare State. Maggie is said to see the working class as 'idle, deceitful and bloody-minded'.(Unlike the upper classes, of course, who are hard-working, honest and straight as they come.)

Advisors report that she was very ignorant about foreign policy. They just about managed to stop her invading Poland and blowing up Russia. Her view seemed to be determined by anti-Communism and the Russian news agency Tass called her the Iron Lady, although I think she got Denis to do the domestic stuff.

Maggie's policies were stunningly successful – if you were one of the few millionaires in England. By 1982 there had been the biggest fall in manufacturing since 1939 and the biggest collapse in production since 1921. Her colleagues complained that she wouldn't listen to them and that she refused to treat them as human beings or even as men, but she refused to listen, gave them sixpence each and told them to run along.

One of the highlights of her reign of terror was the Brixton

'Maggie is said to see the working class as "idle, deceitful and bloody-minded". (Unlike the upper classes, of course, who are hard-working, honest and straight as they come)'

riots, although she insisted they had nothing to do with her policies at all. In fact she showed herself to be very sympathetic to ethnic minorities in a speech about Britain being swamped by them.

This local excitement wasn't enough for our Maggie though, and, when Argentina invaded the Falklands, she said in a speech that it was exciting to have a crisis. Well, there's nothing like a good war to cheer you up, is there?

Victory went to Thatcher's head (and she was fairly potty before). She started to see herself as Queen Margaret and began blaahing on about Victorian values. Accordingly, some of her ministers did what Victorian gentlemen did and shagged anything that moved.

Thatcher did manage to talk her philandering minister Cecil Parkinson into staying with his wife, however, although 'talking into' in her book probably involved a slap round the back of the legs and no pocket money for a week.

Margaret is nothing if not an unpredictable and interesting

> **'On a visit to a factory she said to one of the lads working there, "What an enormous tool you've got." As everyone giggled hysterically, like we British do at a knob joke (and thank heavens or I'd be out of a job), she sailed on oblivious, wondering if she had a biro mark on her face'**

personality. Her favourite Christmas reading would be a 3,000-page report on the siting of a third London airport. I suppose she made the right choice if it was that or an Archer potboiler.

One of her most heinous crimes was lack of a sense of humour. On a visit to a factory she said to one of the lads working there, 'What an enormous tool you've got.' As everyone giggled hysterically, like we British do at a knob joke (and thank heavens or I'd be out of a job), she sailed on oblivious, wondering if she had a biro mark on her face.

A Spanish tourist curtseyed in front of her once, to which she responded, 'Don't do that to me, dear, I'm only in politics.' Perhaps she shouldn't have had the crown on. Her regality surfaced again when she said, 'We are a grandmother.' Of course she may have meant her and Denis, who did look a bit like a grandma at this point.

Eventually Maggie's own party got tired of being pushed around by a woman (even one with more balls than the lot of them). But Maggie didn't take the leadership challenge seriously. She couldn't believe any of those stalking horses could make it to the winning post. Even when the cause was lost, she promised to fight on; she couldn't hear how ridiculous she sounded because as usual she wasn't listening.

Margaret shed a few tears on leaving Downing Street because she hadn't completed her task. There were still some people in work.

She surprised everyone by buying a house in Dulwich instead of moving to Bolivia with the rest of the Nazis. Now she's wandering round the world doing what she does best...lecturing people.

JESUS
Christ

Jesus judges a fat baby competition

Nice orb, shame about the crusades

esus was born before his time. His birth is esti-
mated at 6BC, which is his first miracle. Another
miracle that happened much later was that recently women
were allowed to become priests. I actually predicted this in a
dream I had a couple of years ago. I dreamed I was at the Last
Supper. (I always like to think about noshing, even when I'm
asleep.) Jesus was handing out the bread, saying, 'This is my
body, eat this in memory of me.' Then he gave out the wine
saying, 'This is my blood, drink this in memory of me.' At this
point I piped up and said, 'Isn't there anything for pudding? I'm
bloody starving back here.' Of course that's ridiculous,

because there weren't any women present at the Last Supper. This is why the Church was against women priests, because none of Jesus's disciples were women. Well, none of Jesus's disciples lived in total luxury or was described as 'randy', but that doesn't seem to have stopped current churchmen behaving that way.

'I thought my favourite carol went:
'Away in a manger, no crib for a bed,
The little Maltesers lay down
their sweet heads.'
And I have worshipped chocolate ever since'

Everyone knows the story of Jesus's birth inside out, due to endless scenarios at primary school involving precocious little nippers whose proud parents can barely contain their excitement, until their child wets itself or falls over the donkey. I was in the nativity play at school. For some reason I always got picked to play Bethlehem.

Women figure quite strongly in the life of Jesus, despite the fact that until recently we weren't allowed to deliver the sacrament. Must be the first time some of those men get to serve food. First of all there is the Virgin Mary who is always dressed in blue – I find it hard to believe she is a Chelsea supporter. I suppose the Christian Church should be grateful that Mary wasn't a career woman and actually decided to have the baby.

For quite a while as a child I was confused about the Christian faith because I thought my favourite carol went:
Away in a manger, no crib for a bed,
The little Maltesers lay down their sweet heads.
And I have worshipped chocolate ever since.

The Bible does tell us several stories about women. Jesus never had a girlfriend, but then again I don't know many women who would go out with men who wear sandals. He couldn't have been gay, though, because that would have been blasphemous and therefore against the law.

One story which is very well known is the one of the woman who anointed Jesus's feet in the house of Simon the Pharisee. This woman was reputedly a sinner, which in Biblespeak normally means a prostitute. The woman went into Simon's house and anointed Jesus's feet with oil, wept over them and dried them with her hair – something Sinead O'Connor couldn't manage. Of course Simon started moaning about this because he didn't like having old tarts in his nice clean house. Things haven't changed much, have they? I hate it on the news when they report the murder of 'innocent' women, because this means that prostitutes are guilty women. Bloody hell lads, they're only trying to make a living and keep the more unsavoury of you off the rest of us.

Jesus was also well-known for his miracles and probably would have formed a band if Smokey Robinson hadn't done it. Lots of Jesus's miracles involved food, including the loaves-and-fishes one, and turning water into wine. After he did this one he had to have a quiet lie-down while all the other guests celebrated, except the bloke with a towel round him whose bath was now full of Château Messiah.

I have a lot of respect for Jesus. He lost his temper only

'Jesus was also well-known for his miracles and probably would have formed a band if Smokey Robinson hadn't done it'

once, when he turned over the tables of the money-lenders in the temple, which obviously did the trick because I've never seen any in the temple near my flat.

Jesus was also bang on the side of poor people. In his parables, poor people tended to be the heroes. In one parable he said the widow's mite was a more valuable gift than the money of a rich man because it was all she had. I'm not sure what a mite would be worth today, but I can guarantee that it wouldn't be enough to impress those posh Surrey women collecting for charity.

Jesus suffered because he was too nice and eventually he was sent up before the beak. When he stood before Pilate, the Governor asked him: 'Are you the King of the Jews?' and Jesus answered: 'My kingdom is not of this world.' This is why,

'Mary M followed Jesus everywhere but didn't get into the team due to lack of testicles'

to this day, the leader of the largest Christian Church has to be head of state of an independent country, filled with the greatest collection of riches on the planet, which issues its own postage stamps and dresses its guards in cast-offs from Vivienne Westwood's 1990 collection.

Since Jesus's main aim in life was radically to reform the Jewish religion, I expect he would have been reasonably happy that a religion was set up in his name which spent two thousand years persecuting and murdering Jews with psychopathic zeal. AN Wilson, whose book on Jesus caused many ripples on fusty old churchmen's bowls of porridge, says, 'Few of the Christian churches have ever viewed the teaching of Jesus with anything but contempt.' You can't help but agree with the man.

When Jesus died, all the women round the cross were called Mary. His mother Mary, her sister Mary, and Mary Magdalene (or Mawdlin if you're an Oxbridge wanker). Mary M followed Jesus everywhere but didn't get into the team due to lack of testicles.

As I said earlier, Jesus told the disciples to think of the bread as his body. And he wasn't joking because, when they took him down from the cross, they covered him with a cloth and within three days he was risen.

Jesus was a good bloke, who learnt his lesson the hard way. This lesson is that lots of people in the world aren't very nice. If the Church really did follow the teachings of Jesus, I think people would have quite a good life, but the New Testament seems to be about as relevant to the current Church as Rosemary Conley's work-out video is to me. If Jesus died for our sins, I think it's about time he came back again and had another sort out. It would be a great revelation to me to meet the world's first true new man.

Nice halo, shame about the Inquisition

CHRISTOPHER
Columbus

Chris was a keen collector of mirrors from 'Acorn Antiques'

hris's real name was Christopher Colon but I don't want to put you off your dinner, so we'll stick to Columbus. He came from very humble beginnings and was always keen to advance himself and hide the fact that he was dead common.

In fact, the sailors that worked for him said all he wanted was to be a great lord. In Chris's day the only way of being upwardly mobile was either through the Church or by being a soldier of some kind. Chris, because he wasn't very bright, thought he would do it by being a sailor.

Chris did not have a classical education and taught himself, so there were big gaps in his knowledge. He managed to bluff his way fairly successfully through Trivial Pursuits until he got a literature question.

One thing Chris also did to get on was to marry someone quite rich called Doña Filippa. She gave him lots of cash and died quite young which he didn't seem to mind too much. He did have a few affairs and was particularly in love with a woman called Beatriz Enriquez. However she was a bit downmarket and, although he had a son by her, he wouldn't marry her. Sounds like a right wanker already, doesn't he?

Chris gradually formed the idea in his mind of being an explorer. Not cheap and you did need someone to dosh you up for all the ships, crew and sea-sick pills. Chris pursued Ferdinand and Isabella, the King and Queen of Spain, until they agreed to give him the required amount of money. It was touch and go, though, because he didn't wash his hands after he'd been to the toilet and dropped his aitches all the time. Chris said he would go to India but instead of going east he would go west. At that time no one knew America was in the way. We certainly know now. In fact you know even without stepping outside your front door there are so many crappy detective shows on. Chris set off on his first expedition, taking beads and glass and other naive things to trade with, thinking he'd be able to con the natives.

One problem he had on board his ship, the *Santa Maria,* was telling the time. This was done by getting some poor boy to sit by an hour glass and turn it at regular intervals. As we know, young boys get bored and so we have no real idea how long the journey took because the ship's boy was either off having a slash or using it to see what time the football was on.

One thing Chris was terrified of, apart from being shown up in

118

a discussion about modern art, was mutiny. It's easy to imagine all the crew being stuck on the ship with just a few Rich Tea biscuits and some dried fish to eat getting a little bit irate when they realised no one knew where the hell they were going. In order to calm them down, Chris falsified the ship's log so they wouldn't catch on that all was not well.

Eventually they spotted land, but the first island Chris landed at can't be identified from his description. Besides, he had already lied to the crew, so for all we know, it could have been anywhere. This island was lush and populated with friendly natives...not the Isle of Dogs, then. Chris realised that the natives were exploitable and easily duped but, being a Christian, decided to try to catholicise them (I think I'd rather be exploited and easily duped). Chris kicked off his grand plan by building a garrison and, when he returned to Spain, left about thirty men there to run it. All the explorers had been hoping to find loads of gold and exotic thingummyjigs on their travels but the island yielded up a teeny-weeny bit of Ratners standard gold and some crappy spices that even Colonel Sanders would have turned his nose up at.

The natives did, however, introduce the Europeans to the hammock. And, if the Europeans had been too stupid up to this point to tie some knotted rope to two trees, then they deserved it instead of treasure. I've never been on a hammock. My local council always considered it too dangerous and wouldn't give me planning permission.

Chris returned to Europe a year after he had set sail. At this point he was starting to behave a bit oddly.

'Excuse me sir, I've just spotted a "Welcome to Tenerife" sign'

Feeling lonely, he turned to God, who obviously thought he was a bit common too and helped him out by whipping up a big storm not far from home. The ship managed to get through the storm and landed at the Azores, where some of the crew, going to give thanks at a local church, were clapped into irons, which can be quite painful if they are on and turned up to the 'linen' setting. Chris managed to rescue these men; they were a bit shaken but their shirts looked well pressed. He moved on to Portugal where he was arrested by the King, who was jealous because he had turned down the opportunity to invest in Chris's adventure and thought he might be missing out on some booty. Kings, eh? They're all the same. Chris finally got back to the King and Queen of Spain and, remembering to

120

'This is known as a potato, and you are all hideously ugly'

speak in his plummiest voice, told them of his adventures. Even though he had brought them back a load of old tat, they were confident that, if he went back again, he would eventually return with something decent.

Chris did return, searching for the mystery continent he was sure was in the way. In the Caribbean he was shocked to meet cannibals but, being the *nouveau riche* snob he was, was more shocked that they didn't use knives and forks to eat each other with. When he arrived back at the fort he had built, he found it had been burnt down and all the men he had left there were killed. The Spaniards and the natives blamed each other. Funnily enough, Chris was inclined to believe it was the natives' fault. For good measure, some time later he ordered the execution of a native chief. Chris the Christian was starting to lose it.

Jo Brand – A Load of Old Balls

Chris was still trying to prove that where he was was part of Asia. Rather than making sure using maps and brain, he got all his crew to sign a document supporting this lie with threat of tongues being cut out. And he was upset by cannibals?

Chris and his mates were a real tonic for the natives. They sent slaves to Spain who died in droves on the way. They killed locals with diseases brought from Europe. Then they discovered America and that, as far as I'm concerned, was the beginning of the end of the world. People love America and say it's better than England. I look at it this way. Their top boxer is an ex-mugger and convicted rapist and ours is Widow Twankey in Margate. Which would you rather have? Chris, I wish you'd kept it to yourself.

Chris won the Indians' confidence with his brilliant portrayal of the ugly sisters in Cinders

GEORGE *Best*

Women loved George so much they would even let him keep that sweater on during sex

George loved horses and often practised dressage moves on the pitch

orgeous George (for he is) was born in 1946 into a working-class Protestant family in Belfast. His father worked at the Harland and Wolff shipyard. In those days, he says, the 'Troubles' were under control and Catholics and Protestants lived together on the Cregagh, a vast estate. Nowadays Harland and Wolff has had it and the troubles appear to be well and truly here to stay. George says he had a happy childhood. He liked school and was good at sport. Bloody good job too, methinks.

George remembers quite a lot of fights. I don't know any schoolboy that doesn't. One big boy started hurting him badly, so he rubbed his arm on some broken glass. With big boys you

always had to introduce a weapon to even up the size margin. The boy ran away crying. His dad came round and Best's dad threatened him. That's the sort of dad you want. Perhaps I know a bit too much about fighting for a girl, but I had two brothers whose imaginary friends were called J Edgar Hoover and Klaus Barbie and their idea of going out to play was to lure me into the woods with a sherbert fountain and kick the shit out of me.

George went to a grammar school which was on the edge of a Catholic area, and therefore it was a nightmare getting to and from school. As soon as the Catholic kids saw his uniform, they were genetically programmed to give him a good kicking. He had to time his run to the bus stop. He understandably got fed up with this. I'd have got fed up with it after a day. He started to play truant but needn't have worried because he was brilliant at footy and was about to be lifted out of Belfast and dropped into Old Trafford. (The Manchester United Ground. O, ye girls and boys of little football knowledge.)

'Unfortunately, in the 60s and 70s, clothes shops were called boutiques, which was enough to stop you going into them'

Initially George loved the fame. He was flattered by autograph hunters and kept a scrap book. He bought a car and started with an Austin...aah! how sweet. Then he cottoned on that he was a bit of a playboy, so he gave the car to his dad and bought a Lotus. Then

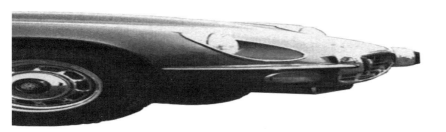

he bought a succession of E-types. The way to tell whether a car is really fashionable is if, as the price goes up, it gets more shaped like a penis.

George also opened a clothes shop. Unfortunately, in the 60s and 70s, clothes shops were called boutiques, which was enough to stop you going into them. You didn't need the discouragement of lime-green crushed-velvet suits and flowery loons on top. George was also just the right age to catch the new age of sexual liberation and free lurve that was being ushered in by the pill and he took advantage of it to the full. He was good-looking, he was famous, he was athlet-

> **'He was good-looking, he was famous, he was athletic and he was rich and we women were queueing up to give him a seeing to'**

ic and he was rich and we women were queueing up to give him a seeing to. I would have had a bash but I was only nine at the time and my mum wouldn't let me wear tights, let alone go and try and get off with George Best.

George says regretfully, 'If in the end I became a monster I did give people pleasure for years before that.' I hope to give people pleasure while I'm a monster.

Although George Best was perhaps one of the most brilliant players in history, it was his antics off the field that people talked about. He tended not to have a reputation as a thug on the pitch, even though he was wound up by other players. He

Jo Brand – A Load of Old Balls

relates one incident in his autobiography when a Yugoslavian goalkeeper dug his nails into his back and threatend to do him after the match. (And I thought it was only girls who used their nails.)

He also says it's hard to keep your cool if someone 'pulls your hair or calls you a masturbator'. Masturbator is a posh book-type word for wanker, I assume, unless Yugoslavian goalies learn all their insults from the OED.

Because George was getting a real reputation as a Lothario, Matt Busby suggested he get married. George took the advice immediately and had a girl from Denmark that he had met once flown over and installed in a flat. This was because she was 'pretty and had a nice figure'. Come on girls, don't look so outraged. Don't kid yourselves he liked her personality. A week later they got engaged and then he dumped her because he was bored. Rule Number One: if you don't want a bloke to get bored with you, either don't sleep with him as soon as you meet him, or learn the League Tables off by heart going back to 1889.

At this point George was drinking very heavily and didn't feel it was worth going to training. I don't even feel it's worth going to the front door when I've got a hangover, so I know how he felt.

The next few years were a mêlée of Miss Worlds and benders. The Miss Worlds were of course something a lot of ordinary women could never aspire to. Loads of people say, 'Huh, the girl next door is prettier than Miss World.' Strangely enough my next-door neighbours never said that. I think the reason George got off with so many Miss Worlds was probably a law-of-averages phenomenon. He'd nomped so many women that a few of them were bound to be Miss Worlds.

For example, George relates going out with a mere Miss Great Britain one night and discovering on arriving at a table with eight women on it that he had shagged all of them. I reckon if I'd been the only one there he hadn't slept with I'd have been in with a real chance. George and his mates played lots of laddish games. For example, if they were all at it in the same

128

house they had to shout 'Geronimo' when they came. Doesn't mention what the women had to shout. 'Bloody miracle!' I would imagine.

One thing about George is he did always tell women the truth. For some women, though, the words 'I'm a complete bastard' just attract them more. I used to be a bit like that. These days I'd rather put my feet up...I can't be bothered, either, to get worked up about George Best's sexual exploits. Most women these days aren't stupid enough to think that blokes are these caring, sharing, little loves that just want to respect us. We know that under the surface of most new men lurks a lad looking to pull. At least when it's on the surface you know what you're dealing with.

United failed to get approval for the
new penalty rule of throwing the striker
into the goal

GAUTAMA
Buddha

Eventually aerobics gets so boring you turn to stone

A Pink Floyd inflatable crash-lands at Battersea Power Station

'm not much cop at impressions but every time I take my clothes off, spray myself gold and have a sit down I am the spitting image of Buddha. There the similarity ends, I'm afraid. For a start Buddha was a man and a very privileged one at that. He was born in 563BC around the time Barbara Cartland was thinking about buying anti-wrinkle cream. He was a royal prince who lived in the lap of luxury, which in 563BC meant he probably had a detached hut instead of a terraced one. At the age of 16 Buddha married and all looked set fair for a fab life of parties, polo and talking to plants.

133

But our Buddha wasn't happy. Very unusually for a Royal, Buddha could not handle the pain and suffering of ordinary people, so he decided to do something about it.

'Buddha thought that worldly life cannot give final happiness. He forgot to mention that beer, fags and Pepperamis can ease the pain a bit'

Rather than wandering round in a carriage looking for some poor old tramp to pull out of a pond in the hope that everyone would love him and not care how much money he'd spent on new pants that week, he decided to become a penniless wanderer himself.

Between feeling sorry for poor people and deciding to wander off, however, over ten years passed. This can only be explained by assuming that he spent a lot of time piling on the calories in preparation for his long ramble without much grub.

Buddha thought that there was more to life than transitory pleasures and that worldly life cannot give final happiness. He forgot to mention that beer, fags and pepperamis can ease the pain a bit.

He wandered about trying to find the meaning of life, thus starting the trend which has drawn thousands of desperate hippies to Nepal and India in the vain hope that, if they see a lot of beggars and go to the toilet involuntarily every three minutes, they'll be able to settle down to life as a DSS counter assistant.

Buddha originally believed that asceticism was the answer, so he had a go at fasting and self-mortification. (We've all done it – for about a millisecond.) Buddha found this method very unsuccessful. (Are you listening, Barry Bethell, with your glass of Slimfast and your smug expression?) Buddha said all this fasting 'clouded his brain'. Perhaps that's why supermodels talk bollocks.

Gautama Buddha

'Well it's an improvement on the usual 24-hour car park'

So for Buddha it was back to noshing and more thinking. He sat under a fig tree and had a long think all night and then it came to him...Buddhism! Hurrah! although what he was doing sitting under a fig tree (eugh, healthy fruit!) I don't know.

Buddha established Four Noble Truths:

Life is unhappy.

Cause of unhappiness is selfishness and desire.

This can be brought to an end by Nirvana. (Like your speakers if you play their records at full volume.)

We can only escape from selfishness by taking the eight-fold path.

Not many laughs there then.

My four noble truths would be:

Men will fight each other for any old reason because they are bastards.

Nice people get trodden on by horrible people.

Women are generally nicer and less violent than men.

135

Jo Brand – A Load of Old Balls

You can't get quicker than a Quikfit fitter.

(I think that last one needs a bit of work.)

Armed with his Four Noble Truths, Buddha went walking around for the next forty-five years preaching his philosophies. None of his preaching was written down at the time but was passed down the centuries by word of mouth. We all know how unreliable Chinese whispers can be, so it's very possible that Buddha said, 'I've got four pairs of shoes,' and that it ended up as, 'I've got four noble truths'. Still Buddha's followers were so poor that, if they'd had any shoes, they'd probably have eaten them.

Buddhists believe in a repeating cycle of births, death and rebirths according to one's physical and mental actions, so nip out and tread on a big fat cockroach because, if Buddhists are right, you might just get Robert Maxwell. Bit pointless, though, because he'd just come back as a big fat cockroach again.

Lots of people tend to see Buddhist philosophy, with its pacifist approach, as a bit of a joke but when you see Buddhist monks wandering around with a serene expression on their faces, they certainly look a lot more sorted out than your average sour-faced, money-obsessed city types. And how many city boys' frocks can you borrow for that special night out at the disco?

Even statues have to have a sit down sometimes

136

JULIUS Caesar

Julius Caesar with his famous detachable todger

Caesar always wore a model of Mrs Thatcher on the front of his shirt

aesar's full name was Gaius Julius Caesar but he didn't use it because he thought it made him sound sissy. He was born into a famous and wealthy patrician family, but he had connections with the riff-raff side of the family who didn't speak to the patrician lot because they were too posh.

As soon as Caesar was old enough he left Rome and went off on his travels. He was once captured by pirates and held to ransom. Kidnapping was popular in those days although it took the family quite a long time to get the ransom note.

Jo Brand – A Load of Old Balls

Caesar joked with his captors that, as soon as he was free, he would buy some ships, capture the pirates and crucify them. As soon as the money was paid, he did just that. A man of his word, obviously, and a complete tosser. Bet those pirates

'Caesar married the cousin of the statesman Pompey, who was honoured by having a football team named after him'

found it hard to see the joke.

After the death of his wife in 68BC Caesar married the cousin of the statesman Pompey, who was honoured by having a football team named after him. Caesar was a Pompey supporter and was given the job of aedile (officer in charge of public buildings). He spent huge amounts of money on games and races to get in with the populace and is attributed with the famous phrase 'Panem et circenses', which means give the punters bread and races. No doubt the punters would have preferred Cakem and Gladiatores but they were happy enough with a sandwich and a bit of juggling.

In 61BC Caesar was sent to Spain as military governor to learn the art of war. I wouldn't call it an art; I'd call it the human relations equivalent of woodwork CSE, but I'm only a girl, so what would I know? On his return Caesar got the top job of consul and he got together with Pompey and Crassus as a triumvirate to achieve mutual political aims. From what I know about men cooperating, two's company, three's bloody pointless.

Caesar then spent about seven years conquering Gaul and Belgium and eventually came to Britain.

140

He is quoted, wrongly, as saying 'Veni, Vidi, Vici', which loosely translates as 'oh dear, oh dear, oh dear'. As Caesar campaigned, he kept a diary of the war, *De Bello Gallico*, to be published as propaganda when he returned to Rome. It was turned down by most publishing houses because there wasn't enough sex in it.

By now Pompey was jealous of Caesar's successes. Well I never. Pompey tried to have Caesar's army disbanded but Caesar led his men back into Italy, crossing the Rubicon river with the phrase 'Iacta alea est', which means 'Kiss my arse, Pompey'. (My own translation.) Needless to say, civil war followed. Caesar thrashed Pompey and became dictator of Rome. He got up too many peoples' noses, however, and was murdered on 15 March, 44BC. A soothsayer had warned him about this but he didn't know what 'the Ides' meant either.

Caesar was very vain. His biographer Suetonius writes: 'He was rather a dandy. He couldn't stand his baldness, which his enemies made fun of, so he used to brush his thin hair forward. Of all the honours he accepted, the one he used most

Caesar wore a dress for easy access

Sheets were popular in those days. Duvets weren't quite so easy to wear

'Not conquering Britain was Caesar's only military failure. Obviously Britons shouted "Spamhead" the loudest'

gladly was the right to wear a laurel wreath on his head at all times.' More interesting than a toupee, I suppose.

Not conquering Britain was Caesar's only military failure. Obviously Britons shouted 'Spamhead' the loudest. Caesar came here twice and intended to occupy the island but the situation got dodgy in Gaul and he had to make do with British tribute and hostages. As soon as decently possible, the Brits stopped paying, ignored Rome and got on with what they are best at – moaning about how crap their football team is and eating kebabs.

Caesar could be brutal and barbaric on occasions, but by Roman standards this made him a bit of a wet. When Gaul rose in revolt, rebels held out in the town of Uxellodunum. Caesar cut off their water supply and, when the rebels surrendered, he had their hands cut off as a public warning. They were

Julius Caesar

'Caesar was considered sexually promiscuous even by Greek, Roman and Paddy Ashdown's standards'

probably fed up with getting gloves every Christmas anyway.

Caesar was considered sexually promiscuous even by Greek, Roman and Paddy Ashdown's standards. He always found time for a bit of shafting regardless of the consequences. He was at it with Pompey's wife when it could have destroyed his political career. When has that ever worried a penis? His affair with Cleopatra scandalised Rome. She is supposed to have been smuggled into Rome in a rug. When she jumped out, Caesar put it back on his head. Even Caesar's soldiers sang the song:

Home we bring our bald whoremonger.
Romans, lock your wives away.

All the bags of gold you lent him
Went his Gallic tarts to pay.

I'm sure I've seen a film of Gazza singing that in a karaoke bar.

Caesar was bisexual and was described as 'every man's wife and every woman's husband'. Nobody really minded, though, because he was a bloke, although the local livestock got a bit twitchy if they saw him coming.

Gaius Julius Caesar: the Greatest Roman – or Baldy Power-Mad Sex Maniac? I'd plump for the latter because I think Gino Ginelli is probably the greatest Roman.

ALBERT Einstein

Before the Nobel Prize brought him financial security, Einstein depended on bit parts in St Trinian's films

Crippled by the costs of his physics experiments, Albert turned to Bingo calling

lbert One-Jug (well, that's the English translation) was born in Germany in 1879. He attended high school in Switzerland (long way to go, but well worth it for the chocolate) and became a Swiss citizen in 1900.

Despite the chocolate I wouldn't have been tempted. For a start, women only got the vote there in the 70s, which is why yodelling was allowed to go on untrammelled for so long. The only good thing about Switzerland is that the tune which precedes announcements in Geneva airport is the first six notes of 'How Much is that Doggie in the Window'.

Jo Brand – A Load of Old Balls

In 1905 Einstein got a PhD, thus qualifying him for a mention in Ian Dury's song, 'There Ain't Half Been Some Clever Bastards'. But, despite being intelligent and qualified to the point of a candidate on Mastermind whom you'd like to punch, Einstein was unable to get an academic position. This may well have been to do with his appearance. He had long shaggy hair and a bushy moustache and looked like he kept loose change in his eye sockets. Eventually he managed to get a job in the patent office in Berne, examining patent applications. So there is a more boring job than being David Mellor's hairdresser.

'He had long shaggy hair and a bushy moustache and looked like he kept loose change in his eye sockets'

Within five years, Einstein had produced four papers which astounded the world of science. Unfortunately they didn't astound me at school because, as a girl, I was unconsciously instructed not to be interested in physics; so, while they were telling me about it at school, I was wondering whether my mum would allow me to wear tights to the school disco. It was a generally accepted scientific theory in those days that gorgeous boys didn't look at you twice if you had long white socks on.

Einstein kicked off his shattering revelations to the scientific world with his Special Theory of Relativity, after he had dispensed with his Dodgy Theory of Relativity and his Quite Nice but Very Ordinary Theory of Relativity. This one, like Special

Brew, will knock your head off.

When I first heard E = MC^2 I was shocked, as I'm a keen Scrabble player and couldn't understand why a mere vowel should be worth so much.

Einstein came up with a lot of revolutionary ideas that other scientists hadn't considered, one of which is that space is curved. Any Special Brew drinker could have told him this.

His Special Theory of Relativity led on to his General Theory

'he was well on the way to being responsible for an equation that could blow the world to kingdom come. And I don't mean a chicken vindaloo washed down with 12 brandies'

of Relativity. If you want to know what this is about, watch Tomorrow's World. Most girls don't, because they never have anything about make-up on it.

Einstein won the Nobel Prize in 1921. Not the Peace Prize, though, because he was well on the way to being responsible for an equation that could blow the world to kingdom come. And I don't mean a chicken vindaloo washed down with 12 brandies.

Hitler was not a big fan of Einstein because he was Jewish. So, when the Nazis came to power, Albert decided to get the hell out of Europe and emigrated to America, where he became Professor of Really Difficult Stuff at Princeton University.

Einstein is described as gentle and humorous. He is supposed to have been full of benevolence and integrity. Bit of a shame then that he was responsible for the creation of nuclear weapons – in Freudian terms, the ultimate penis substitutes. Aha! I hear you say. It's not his fault he only gave the rest of the world the theories to work on. I must say, if I'd been Einstein, I'd have been tempted to keep my gob shut. He was genetically unable to, though, because he was a bloke. There is also the small matter of Einstein urging Roosevelt to sort himself out with nuclear weapons.

'If I'd been Einstein, I'd have been tempted to keep my gob shut. He was genetically unable to, though, because he was a bloke'

Einstein is said to have summed up his outlook on the world by saying, 'God is subtle but he is not malicious'. So God made man in the opposite image to Himself then.

Perhaps Einstein never intended his work to be put to evil use, but as per usual the less savoury types were quite happy to develop nuclear weapons to back them up when they stuck their tongues out at people. The cynical view is that, if we hadn't had the bomb, the world wouldn't be as peaceful as it is today. Oh, is it? I hadn't noticed.

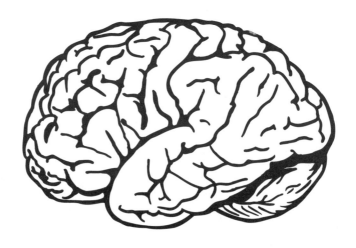

TAKE *That*

Take That...stupid look off your faces

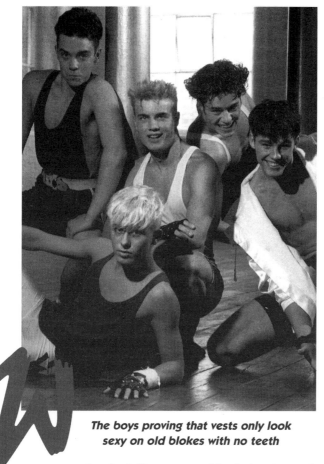

*The boys proving that vests only look
sexy on old blokes with no teeth*

e're just five normal lads having a laugh.'

Yes, that's what worries me, boys. I have never been a big fan of 'lads'. Individually lads are easier to handle but once they get together in a group, the hooligan mentality takes over. And 'having a laugh' means they're off, leaving enraged women in their wake, who wish they had Armalites. I think women should be armed, because then we could go out at night safely, shoot rapists, shoot muggers and shoot anyone else that got on our nerves.

The most pleasant group of lads I have met recentl, recognised me at a 24-hour garage at about two o'clock in the

153

morning. I could tell by looking at them they didn't want my autograph or the opportunity to discuss Andrea Dworkin's anti-pornography campaign. I was right. They proceeded to shout a few witty insults at me such as 'You are an elephant'. Unfortunately, I was with a bloke and therefore knew, according to the Rule Book Of Lads, that, if I retaliated, it would be him who got his head kicked in, not me. So I fixed a grin on my chops and fantasised about using their testicles as a Black and Decker Workmate.

Surely the lads in Take That never behave like this, though? All lads behave like this at some time or another, because that is one of the requirements of being a lad.

'Jason was brought up as a Mormon. All he had to do to join Take That was drop the middle 'm''

So, who are the members of this band that have moistened the hankies and other bits of teenage girls, not to mention a few older women who fantasise about the simplicity of sex with younger blokes because you don't have to have a conversation with them?

First of all there is the songwriter Gary Barlow. He used to be the school tough guy. (Fanzines never use words like 'bully'.) Touching to know he was punching a few spotty little herberts in shorts while secretly constructing 'A Million Love Songs' in his bedroom among piles of tissues.

Young boy bands have to suffer the indignity of supplying the press with a million throwaway inane sentences that sum up their attitudes to aspects of their life. Gary says, 'How can anyone enjoy depressing music?' A conundrum I'm sure Take That's fans have been wrestling with for some time.

Gary doesn't think pop stars should voice opinions and thereby hoists himself very successfully with his own petard. He does have some saving graces – he likes Chinese food and Mars Bars. But he ruins this by saying he thinks Madonna is too muscular and he prefers curvy girls with long hair like Kylie

Minogue. Kylie Monogue is not curvy. If you're looking for curvy with long hair, Gary, you should be looking more at the Meatloaf end of the market.

Gary got together with Mark Owen who was a tea boy at Strawberry Studios. Mark wanted to be a professional footballer, but injury stopped him. It shouldn't have stopped him being considered for Graham Taylor's England squad. Only death does that.

Mark doesn't like older fans because, when they ask for your autograph, they 'try and eat half your face'. That's because the hot dogs at Wembley Arena taste like shit.

Mark and Gary formed a band called 'Cutest Rush'. (Yuk.) They also worked as acting extras for Nigel Martin-Smith. Who he? Well, he'd have to be an agent with a name like that. Through Nigel, Mark and Gary met Jason Orange and Howard Donald.

Jason was brought up as Mormon. All he had to do to join Take That was drop the middle 'm'. Jason wants to be Leader of the Labour Party. He's got a nice smile, so all he needs now

'they got so famous they managed to cover a Barry Manilow single without everyone pissing themselves laughing'

is to avoid having any Socialist policies.

Jason hates pollution. Don't we all, Jason? But he likes Madonna and brown sauce. Not together, I assume.

Howard started his working career as a YTS car sprayer. He, too, is worried about the planet. He's also the soppy one. He says he loves the other members of the band so much that, 'if one got hurt, I love them enough to cry'. Nearly makes you want to buy one of their singles, doesn't it?

Finally, there is Robbie Williams. He was also with Nigel Double-Barrel and has appeared in Brookside. I'd like to appear in Brookside to write some decent bloody plots instead of all that guff about the Liverpool Branch Davidians. Robbie dislikes violence and TV comedy. (I should punch him for that.)

Take That got their name from a tabloid picture of Madonna which was captioned 'Take that and party'. Good job they didn't get it from a tabloid picture at some other period of her career or they could have been called 'Big Pointy Tits Simulating Masturbation'.

Surprisingly Take That had trouble getting their career off the ground. They even had to produce their first single themselves, with a video accompanying it, featuring lots of scantily clad models and jelly. (Do you see what I mean about the laddish element?)

After a few setbacks they had screaming girls fainting in their thousands at gigs and they got so famous they managed to cover a Barry Manilow single without everyone pissing themselves laughing.

Like true lads they do love to show their bottoms from time to time, though now they're a bit older they do at least keep their pants on.

I feel sorry for all these little girls who write to them pouring their hearts out and letting their pubescent sexual fantasies run riot on paper. They're lads, they're probably having a good laugh at them or doing the thing young boys in their bedrooms don't want their mums to catch them at. No, not Airfix construction.

MARTIN
Luther

*Martin Luther's friends would hold their hands over his beard and say
'hey, you're Luke from Bros' (try it kids)*

Martin painted his third chin so it looked like a collar

artin Luther was born in Germany in 1483. It is important to bear in mind that at that time Europe was very much under the yoke of the Catholic Church, so any of the men who did something wrong felt guilty, and the women just felt guilty anyway because we're like that.

Martin had a university education and, although his father tried to persuade him to take up law as a career, he became a monk. Not a decent teenage rebellion there, and the first signs that our Martin, despite his enormous influence on world history, was a bit of a dyed-in-the-wool, stamp-collecting type.

Luther did a degree in theology at the University of Wittenberg and was beginning at this time to formulate many grievances against the Catholics. My grievance against Catholics is that they're funnier than us boring old Church of England mob, because they're more fucked up.

'It didn't take much for you to be playing the starring kebab role'

In 1510 Luther went to Rome and was shocked by the behaviour of the Catholic clergy. He thought they were far too wordly and indulgent and was particularly unhappy with a habit they had called 'selling indulgences'. (Not to mention shagging, gambling and burning witches.) 'Indulgences' were like coupons for the remission of sins. The more you bought, the more you could commit sins without punishment. If you had enough money you could get away with murder... (Nowadays all you need is diplomatic immunity but that's another story.) If you paid your money, your time in purgatory might be reduced – a bit like bribing the receptionist at Champney's to smuggle in a couple of pork pies.

Luther got so wound up about the way the Catholic Church was behaving that in 1517 he nailed a list of his complaints on the door of the church at Wittenberg. He could easily have sent the Church a letter but he just wanted to be a drama queen. It was quite a long list containing ninety-five theses, so he'd really thought about it. By this time Luther was starting to deny the authority of the Pope. The Pope didn't cotton on for a while, he was probably too busy appearing on 'Celebrity Heretic'.

The Church, as you can imagine, wasn't at all happy about Martin's ideas and summoned him to account for himself. He was asked to recant, refused and was declared a heretic by the Diet of Worms. Every schoolchild in the country has heard

160

No one liked Barbara Cartland's latest potboiler

of the Diet of Worms, as has every adult, and virtually no one can remember why they have heard of it, except it is a funny name. Most schoolchildren will have had a diet of worms at some point in their lives as it tends to be one of the rather more unimaginative dares that you get asked to do at school and is probably responsible for producing a high number of vegetarians.

Being declared a heretic in those days wasn't a barrel of laughs. It didn't take much for you to be playing the starring kebab role. The Catholic Church didn't muck about, as they demonstrated with the Spanish Inquisition. They burnt more people at the stake than Take That have had offers for sex. They certainly weren't vegetarians; they loved a bit of crackling. Martin Luther avoided the stake because at the time he had a lot of popular support. He had translated the Bible into German, so that anyone could now read it and didn't have to take the Church's word for what was in it. Sadly, though, the new Jackie Collins was selling more. One of Luther's main ideas was that it wasn't just enough for someone to lead a good life...that wouldn't get them into Heaven. He said salvation comes only through faith and the grace of God. Damn, might as well start pushing loads of old ladies in front of the oncoming traffic, then.

Martin also protested against particular Church beliefs and practices. He said there was no such thing as purgatory, so he'd obviously never been stuck behind someone in the post office who was sorting out their car tax, sending a parcel to

Bolivia and talking to the assistant about their piles.

He also denied that the clergy should be celibate. Good one, Martin. He actually got married to a former nun and they had six kids. Well, I suppose nuns have to catch up on lost time. Martin Luther is considered the main man of the Reformation. He was responsible to a great extent for a lot of the wars that followed and very bloody they were too. I don't want to harp on about the irony of the Christian Church being responsible for some of the most appalling atrocities but world history has been a catalogue of groups of people massacring each other because they thought other religions were looking at them funny. If you stop being a grown-up objective type for five minutes it's as plain as a wart on your face. Which was enough to get you basted at gas mark three in Luther's day.

If Martin Luther had been a holy man beyond reproof like Jesus I would have had more respect for him. However, he was very intolerant and ferociously anti-semitic. German, intolerant, anti-semitic? Sounds familiar? Sounds like he paved the way for Adolf.

The church practising Nazi salutes

MUHAMMED

nfortunately, anything I have to say about Muhammed is likely to seriously damage the health of people who work in bookshops.

Vladimir Ilyich
Lenin

Lenin's hobby was shadow puppets, but he couldn't
get the donkey right

This was the nearest Lenin ever got to a smile

enin's real name was Vladimir Ilyich Ulyanov. He was a heavy smoker, so was also known as Vlad the Inhaler. He was born in 1870 in Simbirsk, a town in Russia. According to the books, his father was a loyal government official and schoolmaster, his mum the daughter of a doctor. What a pity his poor old mum couldn't be a person in her own right. My official title in years to come will be daughter of a civil engineer.

Lenin's brother Alex was a radical like Lenin and was executed for his part in a plot to assassinate the Tsar. Everyone was pissed off with the Tsar at the time. He was swanning about with his family, dressed beautifully, eating expensive

169

Russian woodcarvers all thought Lenin had three fingers

food and not seeming to give a toss about the poor people. So having a crack at assassinating him was quite a popular pastime. You'd pack some sandwiches and a bottle of Tizer, go and find a good spot to sit on and when the Tsar passed, take a pot shot at him. Even if you didn't hit him, you'd had a good day out.

England obviously isn't suited to revolution in the same way. We don't seem to mind our Royal Family too much. They fill thousands of column inches, wear nice hats at Ascot and the only serious assault made on the Palace in recent years was by a man who just wanted to sit on the Queen's bed and have a fag. Unfortunately, she'd run out of Capstan Full Strength.

By the age of 23, Lenin had become an ardent Marxist. In 1895 he was arrested by the Tsarist government and spent 14 months in jail. He was then exiled to Siberia where, apparently, he had quite a nice time, even getting his future wife to join him. Must have been some kind of woman. You wouldn't catch me trailing all the way to Siberia for the man I loved. Well, not unless there was a substantial tea at the other end.

They'd had an interesting romance, distributing leaflets

together and talking about the revolution. The sort of romance agony aunts try to persuade you is possible if you go to evening classes. I am convinced no woman ever met a future husband at evening classes. You're about as likely to meet your future husband there as you are to meet him through Dateline.

Lenin legged it from Siberia and spent the next 17 years in Europe – a sort of elongated holiday. He worked as a professional revolutionary. There wasn't a job description, since Lenin invented the title, so he could do anything he wanted.

The problem with Russian Communism has always been the huge gap between the intellectuals, who formulated the theories, and the working classes, who were needed to put them into action. Half the time the proletariat didn't know what the intellectuals were on about. The intellectuals would talk about dialectical materialism and the proletariat would respond by saying: 'Can't we just have some bread and watch Neighbours.' It's even harder in Britain because the revolutionaries say things like: *'Socialist Worker!'* and the proletariat respond with: 'Piss off, I'm

Russian stand-up comics very sensibly carried guns

171

going to buy the *Sun*.' Lenin was very keen on the idea of the dictatorship of the proletariat, but the proletariat weren't sure how to achieve it. Very conveniently, the leaders of the Communist Party helped them out by becoming dictators for them.

Stalin was such a murderous psycho that, in comparison, Lenin doesn't seem quite so bad, but he did say things like: 'Not a single problem of the class struggle has ever been solved in history except by violence,' and 'One ought to encourage the vigour and wholesale character of the terror against counter-revolutionaries.' So Lenin wasn't such a nice bloke either. He warned that Stalin was too ruthless. Mr Pot and Mr Kettle might have been appropriate names for him and Stalin.

Lenin was still in Europe when the Russian Revolution took place, but he returned to Russia when it looked like there might be a chance of the Bolsheviks taking power. Lenin travelled across Germany on a sealed train. This wasn't because he had German Measles, but because he didn't want anyone to suss who he was and send him to Siberia again. When he arrived, however, Lenin discovered that the time wasn't right for him in Russia and he had to leg it off and come back later. (Coming early, a perennial male problem.) Lenin eventually gained power in November 1917.

Like all repressive regimes, the Communists had to have a secret police. They were called the Cheka, 'the hammer of the revolution', and in the first year of their existence they chalked up nearly 13,000 executions. (Aah, bet their mums were proud.) The head of the Cheka was called Dzerzhinsky and his nickname was 'Nasty Piece of Work'.

Lenin got Russia out of the First World War and tried to sort out the economy. He tried a completely socialist economy, but that didn't work so he had to go for a mixed economy, which allowed some private enterprise. (In our society it's the other way around. We are allowed a teeny-weeny bit of Socialist economy, although this does make the Tories cry quite a lot.) The new economy in Russia didn't work brilliantly either, but because Lenin controlled the press, it didn't matter – all the papers said that things were going very well.

Things didn't go very well for Lenin, though. In 1922 he had a series of strokes which left him incapacitated. He died in 1924. Lenin was not only responsible for lots of deaths himself, he also laid the groundwork for Stalin to kill many millions more after his death. In fact, the main disservice Lenin did to Russia was dying at the wrong time. You can't rely on anyone these days, can you?

RONALD
McDonald

Nosh

Ronald McDonald is a cartoon character, a registered trademark and a corporate logo. If he ran for president, he'd be elected. Ronald is taking over our lives.

First of all, think what a clever name he has. You see, Ronald rhymes with Donald, so they had to use it, even though it is a very old-fashioned name. It doesn't seem to have put the kids off, even though he is named after my dad.

If you are a comic you are always told by TV companies to be very careful about doing jokes about McDonald's because they are litigious, so if you're reading this Mr McDonald, I'm only kidding, mate.

Jo Brand – A Load of Old Balls

Ronald's smiling face and yellow dungarees have helped re-educate half the world in their eating habits. Why bother with bananas fried in coconut oil when you can have a greasy disc of emulsified cow in a bap? Wash it down with a large Coke from which the cocaine has been removed for your own safety and you have the ultimate American dining experience. God Bless The United McStates of America.

'Ronald McDonald is a cartoon character, a registered trademark and a corporate logo. If he ran for president, he'd be elected. Ronald is taking over our lives'

As a fat person, going into McDonald's, or indeed any place that sells food, is something of an ordeal. Society thinks that if you are fat you shouldn't eat anything, so you tend to be very aware of the censorious gazes raining down on your back as you move up the queue. By the time you get to the top you feel forced to order a black tea and run out crying.

The name Big Mac is generally supposed to have come about because it's a big McDonald's burger, but in fact it was named after a big raincoat whose tastes it so closely resembles. I have to confess I do like Big Macs, but, then again, I like anything that comes under the heading, 'It's got calories and you can put it in your mouth.'

Ronald McDonald does seem to have wrestled the crown from other popular English eating experiences. Perhaps they went wrong by not giving their eating places a name and a character to identify with. We could have had 'Pimpley Wimpey', the spotty layabout who lures children in with a promise of extra lard and terminal acne.

More Nosh

178

Ronald McDonald

'We could have had "Pimpley Wimpey", the spotty layabout who lures children in with a promise of extra lard and terminal acne'

The golden arches of McDonald's are incredibly popular. One happy couple recently held their wedding reception at McDonald's, prior to a more private congress between his McNuggets and her McMuffin.

McDonald's are expanding all over the capitalist world and almost every week, Ronald dreams up some new ethnic dish to McDonaldise for us. Pity they don't seem to be too heavily into charity or we could be seeing McRice Rations washed down with McDiseased Water.

But each new McDonald's does bring important new jobs to the community, principally among street-sweepers and poor bastards who are good at mumbling, 'Have a nice day,' while simultaneously conveying, 'Piss off you fat cow and go to Weightwatchers.' Each McDonald's sells vegetarian food – all their cows are vegetarians (except for the mad ones and they'll eat anything).

'Eventually, everything will have a "Mc" in front of it from McLager to McPudding. Well McBollocks to that'

Ronald McDonald is certainly more popular with children than other cartoon characters, like Michael Jackson, but I'd like to see a Ronald McDonald adults could identify with, a Ronald who goes for a takeaway after a night on the piss, who smokes in the no-smoking section, puts his fag out in somone's Coke and lurches down the road with a mouthful of styrofoam, dripping mustard and ketchup down his front. He, of course, could be called Old McDonald.

So where is this frenzied consumption of burgers leading

179

us? Well, if America is anything to go by, it seems likely that a few deranged Falklands vets may spray our McDonald'ses with automatic fire as they seem to be popular venues for this sort of behaviour in the States. Proper dinner will become a thing of the past as Ronald McDonald, like a crappy mime version of the Pied Piper, leads us all down the road to heart disease and high cholesterol parties.

Eventually, everything will have a 'Mc' in front of it, from McLager to McPudding. Well McBollocks to that. I'm not usually a supporter of the meat-and-two-veg meal, but if it stops us entering for ever the false and brightly coloured McHell for which we are headed, I'm all for it...The milk shakes are nice, though.

LUDWIG VAN
Beethoven

Ludwig hides the potty for a Hello exclusive

Beethoven tries to make a thick Viennese audience understand which symphony he's about to perform

eethoven was born in Bonn in 1770 and published his first work at the age of 13, leading us to imagine that he must have been a precocious little git. It wasn't really his fault, though. Beethoven's dad was a bit of a piss artist and wanted his son to become a child prodigy because it's a good way to earn beer money, so he forced little Ludwig van to have piano lessons at a very early age. In fact little Beethoven had to stand on the piano stool to reach the keys.

Beethoven was supposed to have been a bit grubby. I was described by the Mail on Sunday as 'grubby' and that's

because I don't bother to wash when I'm meeting some stuck-
-up right-wing journalist for an interview.

Beethoven was a dark brooding presence. He has been
called the Shakespeare of music. Da Da Da Daah – 'To be or not
to be.'

'It was largely because of Beethoven's principled stand that the wearing of powdered wigs by people with hair died out. Of course the only silly donkeys who do it now are judges'

Beethoven was tutored briefly by Mozart and also by Haydn,
who found him unruly, undisciplined and in need of a good
thrashing. Haydn disapproved of Beethoven's intensity. He told
Beethoven that music was no place for dramatic expressive-
ness or indulgent subjectivity. Beethoven nodded, smiled and
reflected that he would have to stop going to these artistic
soirées because he could hardly hear what people were saying any more.

Mozart and Haydn didn't like Beethoven because he refused
to wear a powdered wig. He considered them decadent and
old-fashioned. He said only bald people like Madame de
Pompadour should wear them. After all, you didn't see healthy
people wandering round on crutches. It was largely because
of Beethoven's principled stand that the wearing of powdered
wigs by people with hair died out. Of course the only silly don-
keys who do it now are judges.

Beethoven was quite popular with the nobs in Vienna,
although he wasn't always very polite to them. He gobbed a
lot. He was arrogant. In fact he appears to have been an early
example of a punk. He is quoted as saying to a prince, 'There
will always be lots of princes but there is only one Beethoven.'
So he can't have been a real punk because he got through a
whole sentence without dying of a heroin overdose.

Beethoven contemplates joining Spandau Ballet

Beethoven also annoyed many composers by dumping the minuet in favour of the scherzo, which was much less sedate. To many, a symphony without a minuet was like a court jester without a pig's bladder on a stick. It was unheard of and, as far as they were concerned, it would never work. Beethoven proved them wrong, nine times.

Beethoven was supposed to dedicate his third symphony to Napoleon, but Napoleon crowned himself and ruined everything. Where was the new republicanism that was supposed to take Europe forward to the age of enlightenment? Beethoven scratched Bonaparte's name from the title page, spat on it and rubbed it until it became a grey smudge, then he tore it up, trampled it on the ground and burnt it, all the while screaming with rage. It was a tantrum of such heroic proportions that the symphony could only be called the *Eroica*.

Jo Brand – A Load of Old Balls

Beethoven had a very raucous laugh. This among other things made him difficult to live with and he had terrible problems keeping servants. Consequently his house was always in a right mess. One baron who visited found a chamber-pot under the piano. Thank God for toilets or many bachelors would still be doing this today.

Beethoven also lost his temper easily and once dumped his dinner on someone's head. Silly sod, he could have nipped home and got the chamber-pot. He had good teeth, piercing eyes, pock-marked skin and was five feet four inches tall. (Another shorty trying to prove himself.)

Beethoven never married, although he did ask a few times. Most of his relationships were unsuccessful. It is difficult for us women to get seriously involved with people who honk a bit and don't let us finish our dinner. He dated one of his piano pupils for a while. I considered dating my piano teacher, except she was sixty, I was eight and I only ever got Rich Tea biscuits when I went for my lessons.

Three letters were found after Beethoven's death addressed to his 'immortal beloved'. Problem is no one knows who that was. The letters contain highly senti-
mental declarations of love and com-
plaints about his health. I used to
go out with a bloke who
moaned about headaches.
Perhaps I should have stopped hitting him on the
head with a
baseball bat.
(Har! Har!
Only kid-
ding.)
Beethoven
started to go deaf
at 20 and was com-
pletely deaf by his
40s. This tragedy

186

had only one advantage – he couldn't hear any longer his dad singing 'I'll take You Home Again Kathleen' under his window.

'Poor old bastard, he must be revolving in his grave as fast as the exit turnstiles of a Julio Iglesias concert'

On dying, Beethoven is said to have shaken an angry fist at the heavens, although it's possible, because he was a moody bugger, that he wanted one last punch-up before he went.

Beethoven is said to have moved an audience to tears more than any other musician of his time. These days that accolade has been bestowed, I think, only upon The Baron Knights, not for the same reason, of course.

Beethoven was the first composer to live independently of the patronage of the Church or nobility. Must have been a relief. These days, the only acts that could make it under that system would be The Three Degrees, Phil Collins and Cliff Richard.

Beethoven did write some fabulous music which erudite music lovers are very snobbish about because it is romantic and populist. Those people who don't like classical music because they think it's boring only have to hum along to a few marge adverts to get some idea of what Beethoven wrote. Poor old bastard, he must be revolving in his grave as fast as the exit turnstiles of a Julio Iglesias concert.

When Beethoven died, thirty thousand people attended his funeral (there were no public hangings that day).

NAPOLEON
Bonaparte

*The posture says 'Yes', the face says
'Not tonight Josephine'*

apoleon Bonaparte was born in Corsica in
1769 and when he grew up he attended a
military academy – this of course is a euphemism for, 'He
learned how to become an unfeeling, puerile, aggresive,
hardnut, bastard' (Not unlike most Tory MPs). So the next step
was to go round all his poor neighbours handing out pretty
blankets he had knitted himself. Only joking. The next step
was, of course, non-stop rucking and Napoleon was certainly
up for that.

Despite being a supporter of the Corsican Nationalists he
abandoned them at the drop of a hat. Nice to see traditional
values like betrayal haven't disappeared in politics. Napoleon
made himself very popular at the siege of Toulon, recapturing

it from Britain. (We didn't bloody want it anyway). He was then made commander of the French Army in Italy and became a war hero. However, he wasn't that great because when he took his troops to Egypt, they got completely routed. Still it was a long way so nobody gave a toss. (Bit like Bosnia and Rwanda.)

The Frank Bruno effect was well and truly working for him (except he hadn't got dressed up as Cinderella); within six years he rose to the position of undisputed leader of France. People seem to think that that's not a very long time. If I went to Italy, I could become Prime Minister in the time it takes to say, 'No, I'm not Luciano Pavarotti.'

Once he was top dog Napoleon set about changing things. He created the Bank of France and the University of France and said very clever things like, 'The English are a nation of shopkeepers.' So it was all the more enjoyable when we did him at the Battle of Trafalgar. Have a nice day, Napoleon.

Although he originally kicked off with lofty ideas, Napoleon didn't manage to hang on to them for very long. Despite at first calling himself Defender of the Revolution, he soon decided he wanted to be Emperor of France. So it was, 'Bugger all the poor people, where's me crown and me jewels?'

From then on it was jobs for the *garçons*. He put three of his brothers on three other thrones in Europe and decided he wanted to do a bit more conquering. He got involved in wars he could not win and during the Russian Campaign, the French army was decimated. I play Risk once a year at Christmas and I could have told him not to bother. Russia's a right bugger to invade. But I know why he did it. If you play Risk with boys, you will see that a total bloodlust overtakes them, despite the fact that they've only got three armies left in Chile...it's sad. Especially when they chuck the board on the floor and go down the pub because they've lost.

Napoleon had a big sulk about Russia, and the rest of Europe saw their chance and thrashed him at the battle of Leipzig. At this point Old Boney resigned and was banished to the island of Elba.

After two years he escaped and was restored to power. (Short memories the French, must be all that Perrier.) Then came Waterloo and I'm afraid old Napoleon didn't do as well as Abba with it. We stuffed him again and he was imprisoned by the British on the island of St Helena and that's where he died. Now you might have noticed that I haven't mentioned his personal life at all. Napolen is most famous, I'm afraid, for saying, 'Not tonight Josephine'. So are about twelve hundred men all round the world whom I've attempted to get in the sack.

So who was this Josephine? Well, by all

A RIGHT BUGGER TO INVADE RUSSIA

EGYPT

A GOOD KICKING

accounts she was a right goer. She was born in Martinique and when she arrived in Paris she caused an amazing sensation in French Society, according to the history books. What that actually means, I have no idea. Did she have nicer shoes than

'*Hold on a minute chaps, bit of a problem with the perspective*'

everyone else, a bigger chest or the latest wig headdress with a dry weave top sheet? Whatever it was, Napoleon fell for her in a big way. She'd already managed to get rid of one husband who'd been guillotined for being an unsuccessful soldier. They didn't court martial you and get you a job in Group 4 in those days.

Josephine decided to marry Napoleon when he was put in charge of the French army in Italy. Not a gold-digger then? he sent her dozens of love let-

ters from Italy, which she very rarely answered. Playing hard to get or no stamps, I'm not sure. She also had an affair while Napoleon was in Egypt. That's what I like to see: a man being kicked while he is down.

But Napoleon, being a bloke, tired of her anyway and started saying, 'Not tonight Josephine,' even when she was out at the shops. She began to complain of his increasing callousness, having managed to ignore up to this point all the people his armies had slaughtered in the wars. What a pair...sounds like they deserved each other.

Why did Napoleon behave in the way he did? First of all, by all accounts, he was a bit of a short-arse and you know what they say about small men. They only come up to your Adam's apple and don't like it, so they have to compensate by becoming Emperor of France.

Napoleon is supposed to have been a supreme military strategist, but we've all seen these poor sods with their little armies set out on the living room carpet when their missus is trying to hoover. They're good strategists too – and they've got all the humanity and empathy of a Millwall fan with toothache.

Napoleon...shorty psycho.

NAPOLEON
BONAPARTE

SHORTY
PSYCHO

WILLIAM
Shakespeare

Will writing to his mum explaining that he's had 25 plays produced
and could he now wear long trousers, please?

Shakespeare left his wife his second-best bed but she made him wear coloured shirts with white collars all the time

illiam Shakespeare was born in 1564. He was brought up in Stratford-upon-Avon, which sadly, thanks to him, is now swarming with Americans who wouldn't recognise a quote from Shakespeare if it kicked them in the Two Gentlemen of Verona.

Nothing is known about Shakespeare's childhood, so for all we know he could have been brilliant at school, hopeless at school or not at school at all.

There are no records of his attendance at Stratford Grammar School, so perhaps he was a skiver. Nothing wrong with that: I was a skiver at school too, 'specially when we were doing Shakespeare.

Jo Brand – A Load of Old Balls

Lots of academics think that Shakespeare didn't write his plays and poems anyway. In fact they're not even sure what his real name is. Shakespeare and Shagspeare have both been offered as possibilities. If the latter was his name perhaps that's why he didn't go to school...he was too embarrassed.

Will smokes drugs to look grown-up, but Mum still won't let him wear long kecks

At 18 Shakespeare married Anne Hathaway. I reckon she actually wrote the plays because they all used to say about her: 'Anne Hathaway with words.'

There is no record of Shakespeare's activities between 1585 and 1592. Why not? It's a very long time. He could have been doing anything. People assume he was in London working as an actor, or maybe a school teacher. Considering generations of schoolchildren have been tortured by his work it seems possible he was sadistic enough to make it as a schoolteacher.

At the end of this period London theatres closed for two years because of the plague. I suppose no one would have been too impressed by a Juliet covered in boils, although *Henry VIII* could realistically have gone ahead.

How did our Bill earn his living? People have guessed he had an income from a patron, the Earl of Southampton. At this point he was known as William Sponger.

In 1594 Shakespeare appears in records as an actor. He was part of a group who organised the building of the Globe Theatre. This is such a treasured part of our national heritage that it is not surprising lots of city types have been keen to build a car park on it.

One side of Shakespeare that they certainly don't teach you at school is how rude he is. It's only just beginning to dawn on

200

Will's 'I will wear ladies' stockings' campaign forces Mum to relent, and she sews him a pair of longies herself

me that we could have had so much more of a laugh if we'd had the unabridged versions of the plays. Shakespeare has some brilliant words for women's rude bits including 'box unseen', 'clack dish', 'pillicock hill', 'nest of spicery' and 'constable'. (Constable?)

He's just as good on men's bits with 'potent regiment' and 'potato finger'. (Yeah, I know what he means. I've had experience of the McCain oven chip.)

Shakespeares' plays are divided into comedies and tragedies and normally involve cross-dressing twins who are not even recognised by their relatives. This sort of thing does not appeal to kids of 14 who are considering the merits of *Jackie* and *Viz* or, if they are boys, putting immense strain on their potato finger with soft-porn mags.

201

Jo Brand – A Load of Old Balls

Oscar Wilde always accused Shakespeare of being gay, but then again he probably thought Queen Victoria was and she didn't even know what being gay meant.

In 1612 Shakespeare retired from acting and went back to Stratford. It was not until after he died that everyone started

'I could have had a crack at Falstaff who just gets pissed all the time'

saying he didn't really write the plays. Their main argument was that, because he was a country bumpkin, he wouldn't have had a grasp of the language used in his plays. What they're saying really is that it's the equivalent of Gazza writing *A Brief History of Time*. We know Gazza couldn't have written that because academically he is at the level of a 12-year-old... race horse.

The most favoured contender for the title of Shakespeare is Francis Bacon. One of the theories put forward in support of this is that, in *Love's Labours Lost*, the word 'honorificabilitudinitatibus' is a Latin anagram of, 'these plays are the offspring of F Bacon preserved for the world'. Bit bloody tenuous, isn't it? I suppose supercalifragilisticexpialidocious is a Latin anagram for 'Dick van Dyke...crap Cockney accent'.

Shakespeare did give men all the best parts and in his day all the female characters were played by men anyway – apart from Anne Hathaway, I hope.

A generous man, Shakespeare left Anne Hathaway his 'second-best bed' in his will. He obviously left his favourite bed to some bloke down the road who said he liked one of his plays once. Typical bloody man. If I'd been Anne I would have changed all his plays so they were crap and given all the male parts to women. Then I could have had a crack at Falstaff who just gets pissed all the time.

My favourite Shakespearean heroine is Lady Macbeth, a hyper loony, who went round saying things like 'Out damned spot', so could have done a great advert for Stain Devils or Clearasil, and Portia in *The Merchant of Venice,* who at least gets to say something important instead of just being bunged in so she can snuff it prettily at the end.

Falstaff, or the Lard of Avon

MR
Costakis

Norf London haute cuisine

The perfect man

ou will never have heard of Mr Costakis although he is a hero in my life. Mr Costakis was a Greek Cypriot who owned a kebab house in Finsbury Park in North London, opposite a comedy club called The Red Rose where I used to do loads of gigs.

Despite the fact that most people think I have a cake in my mouth twenty-four hours a day, one of the tragedies of being a comic is that it is very hard, owing to nerves, to eat anything before you go on stage, because of the fear that it will exit, uninvited, from one of your orifices just before your favourite punchline.

Therefore, as soon as a gig had finished, all the comics on the bill (who weren't on drugs) were starving. Fortunately there were three kebab houses opposite The Red Rose and we fixed on Mr Costakis's gaff because one of the others had music loud enough to make you murder children and at the other one we were about as welcome as a mad cow in Germany.

Mr Costakis was an enormous man in his 50s and I felt comfortable in the company of a similarly sized girth. Outside the restaurant, above the window, there was a picture of him in his native environment – sitting at a table in the sun, drinking. He seemed a lot happier in the picture than he looked in Seven Sisters Road, which is a dirty, busy, dangerous road containing grotty shops and The Chip Shop of Hell, so named by me because I always thought I'd get murdered there.

'Mr Costakis was a bit of an old perv'

Eating in Mr Costakis's restaurant was a bit like being in the jungle. Great trailing plants hung down from the ceiling. The telly was always on with the sound down, and, as we were there on Friday nights, we often caught a comedy show with our mates on it and took the piss. Sadly, one night, I appeared on the screen and the two waitresses went bonkers and tried to turn it up. Thankfully the volume control was broken, so I escaped.

Mr Costakis was a bit of an old perv. He would occasionally try and grab bits of your appendages, so you had to manoeuvre swiftly out of the way before he got hold of another bit. He never said much but would grin and grunt a lot, although we realised eventually that he understood English much better than he pretended to.

'Mr Costakis's gaff was the home of endless streams of dodgy North London traders flogging stuff which was destined to be mentioned by Shaw Taylor'

He began giving me little presents, the odd lighter, free drinks. One day, in front of all my friends he presented me with the most hideous fluffy toy I had ever seen in my life. This invited comments from my friends like 'Phworr, you're in there!' and 'These Greek blokes like fat birds, you know.'

Mr Costakis's gaff was the home of endless streams of dodgy North London traders flogging stuff which was destined to be mentioned by Shaw Taylor. One particular guy often popped in with toys that you knew would fall apart as soon as you touched them.

One night, however, he turned up with some brilliant lighters in the shape of fairly realistic guns. I bought a couple in the vain hope that, if I ever got mugged, I could whip one out of my handbag and frighten off my assailant. Even if he got me wallet, at least I could light up a fag afterwards.

Mr Costakis had obviously got fat from eating his own food, which was fab. Everyone else moaned about it because there wasn't much choice but the lamb chops deserved to be knighted.

Jo Brand – A Load of Old Balls

Unfortunately Mr Costakis's body was a kingdom of cholesterol and he died a few years ago. I never got off with him. It's all too easy when someone gives you the come-on all the time. After he died we all drifted away from the place, although I often drive past reliving happy memories I have of great dinners.

Having had a few holidays in Greece and witnessed the sexual appetite of Greek blokes, who are quite happy to take you from behind while your face is sticking in a cactus, even if you're not keen, I know that Mr Costakis wasn't a big fan of Germaine Greer. But I liked the old bugger and, because he was fatter than me, at least I had the chance of legging it off slowly, secure in the knowledge that he was very unlikely to catch me.

GENGHIS
Khan

Genghis's horse was brilliant at back flips

*'Come here and say my hat makes me
look like a big Jessie'*

enghis Khan was born in 1162. His father was
a petty Mongol chieftain in the sense that he
was not very important, rather than that he counted his
change obsessively if someone popped out to get him ten
Number Six.

Genghis wasn't called Genghis originally; he was called
Temujin, named by his father after a defeated rival chieftain.
Not a popular custom these days. You don't meet too many
Saddams or Adolfs (although Margaret is worryingly popular).
Might be an improvement on Beatrice or Eugenie, though.

Jo Brand – A Load of Old Balls

When Temujin was nine his father was killed, which put the boy in great danger from other tribes. This is because it was generally accepted that nine-year-olds cannot fend for themselves, unless of course they have the might of Hollywood behind

'Say what you like about Genghis Khan but, when he was around, old ladies could walk the streets of Mongolia at night and people knew they could leave their doors unlocked when they went out'

them, are called McCauley Culkin and can irritate people to death.

Temujin was kidnapped in a raid by a rival tribe. I doubt very much that they bothered to kidnap little girls because in those days females invited about as much respect as a lump of yak dung, in fact probably less because at least you could use yak dung for a few plugging jobs around the house. (They would probably have used women if they couldn't run away.)

During this time Temujin was forced to wear a wooden collar. It could have been worse; it could have been wooden underpants. (I've got a wooden nightie which doubles up as an aircraft hangar at Heathrow.)

Temujin managed to escape from his captors and allied himself to a bloke called Toghiril, a friend of his father's. What came next I wonder? What always comes next? Rucking a-go-go, of course.

Temujin indulged in many years of fighting and worked his way to the top. 'The top' in those days meant your massacre quotient was very high. Temujin, however, felt that all his work had been a bit pointless because he'd killed only local tribes. As we know, human nature dictates that it's much more fun to kill foreigners.

So Temujin welded all the tribes together and gave them something to really look forward to... going abroad and wiping out greasy wops and the like. Because they were all so happy about getting this opportunity, Temujin was renamed Genghis Khan which means Great Emperor.

Genghis Khan had the manners of a housefly. He and his men didn't bother with chopsticks; they ate with their hands standing up. Anything else would have been considered effeminate. But he also wore a hat that looked like a Biggles helmet, with earflaps to keep his ears warm in the Mongolian desert, so he wasn't that hard.

Genghis destroyed cities so totally that his Mongol hordes could ride over the rubble in the dark without stumbling, as they charged from the Yellow Sea to the Black Sea and back again. In those days Mongolian warriors did all their charging on horseback. Now, like everyone else, they're learning to do it with plastic.

Genghis Khan extended his reach as far as China, Persia, Russia and Afghanistan. He ruled with an iron fist, which he had specially imported from Taiwan.

'Genghis Khan, as far as I'm concerned doesn't mean 'Great Emperor' it means "Ronnie Kray On A Horse"'

Eventually, after years of laying waste to half the world, he became frightened by an unfavourable conjunction of planets, turned back towards his home village and died of illness on the way. What a wimp.

Say what you like about Genghis Khan but, when he was around, old ladies could walk the streets of Mongolia at night and people knew they could leave their doors unlocked when they went out. Eight hundred years later there are still people in Mongolia who remember what a nice bloke Genghis was and how he loved his mum. On the other hand there are also people who remember how he destroyed their local Safeways, killed their family and ate the contents of their freezer.

Genghis Khan, as far as I'm concerned doesn't mean 'Great Emperor' it means 'Ronnie Kray On A Horse.'

KARL Marx

Karl always saved money on his Father Christmas outfit for Selfridges

he name Karl Marx arouses very different feelings in people, from the antagonistic paranoia of rich capitalists to the staunch admiration of *Socialist Worker* vendors. Both are equally irritating if you ask me. *Hello* readers, of course, are totally uninterested because he's dead and his house didn't have a nice kitchen anyway. Lots of people know what Marx said, but few know anything about the man and his background. So who was this man who has wound up the Americans and the Tories so much?

Karl Marx was born in Germany in 1818. His father was a lawyer and his mother was a housewife, rumoured to be virtually illiterate – so she would have been an avid *Sun* reader. Karl

219

had a reasonably normal upbringing and as a child spent much time with the girl who was to become his wife, Jenny, whose family lived nearby. By the time he was 14 he was madly in love with Jenny who was four years his senior and much posher

'Marx became *persona non grata* with the establishment due to his ideas about the working classes deserving a reasonable slice of the cake, which is entirely unreasonable because I want it all'

than him. She called him her 'little wild boar', which suggests he was quite hairy and good at finding truffles.

Karl went to university in Bonn and then Berlin where he spent his time getting drunk and sending crap poetry to his family…typical student, then. He was also arrested for drunkenness and started to get heavily into debt, which resulted in a flood of letters from his dad telling him to sort himself out and a letter from his mum telling him to wash.

Things went from bad to worse and he had what is euphemistically termed a nervous breakdown, more likely a massive hangover, and his parents began to despair of him. He was rejected for military service due to weak lungs (probably from all that sighing and heavy breathing while composing his crap poetry) and, despite his mum begging him to get a decent job, he went into journalism.

Soon Marx became *persona non grata* with the establishment due to his ideas about the working classes deserving a reasonable slice of the cake, which is entirely unreasonable because I want it all. He was chucked out of Paris, where he had been

220

living with Jenny, moved to Brussels and devoted his time to writing. If you want to know what he wrote, go to the library because there's a lot of it and he isn't very good at sex scenes.

Still crap at managing money, he wrote to his mother asking for handouts, which was a bit mean as his poor old mum was a widow trying to support her daughters. Marx and Jenny were arrested in Brussels and from then on were forced to move from country to country getting gradually poorer and more unpopular as they went (a bit like me on a tour of rugby clubs). Following a spell in Cologne and then Paris again, both of which they were forced to leave, they got really desperate and ended up heading for Blighty. Jenny must have been very happy about this. She was ill, seven months pregnant and, when they arrived in London to live in Soho, the place stank and cholera was rife. Good old England, eh? Only the diseases change.

Jenny spent much of the time down the pawnshop and doing other bits of business, because Karl's English was hopeless. She also had to cope with the unwelcome sexual attentions of an officer named Willich. He challenged Karl to a duel but Karl refused to pick up the glove as he had a pair of his own. One of his young enthusiastic supporters felt obliged to do it for him and got shot in the head. (It's all right, he didn't die.) Is there a pattern forming here? Karl's not too hot in the action department, is he? In fact I'd go as far as saying... bit of a lazy old git. 'Workers of the World Unite...while I put my feet up.'

Karl got a reader's ticket for

Karl entered many beard competitions

221

the British Museum and spent a lot of time there, at which point I expect Jenny called him her 'little wild bore'. Finally he did take some action and got the family maid up the duff. His old friend Engels took the rap by passing the child off as his own. Once again he managed to get a mate to do his dirty work for him or, at least, to take responsibility for it.

'you kind of wish his mum had taken a baseball bat to him and got him a job as a milkman'

Karl Marx did produce a tremendous volume of work and is credited as the father of Communism. His theories have been chewed over, worshipped, abhorred and used to suit the purposes of individual personalities, many of them power-mad, cold, murderous, puerile psychos. Unfortunately, idealistic theories which attempt to improve the lot of society have to be interpreted and put into practice by, yes, you've guessed it... men. And men with power can't help being horrible bastards... it appears to be compulsory. I'm sure Karl Marx wasn't a horrible bloke but, from a female point of view, looking at the life his missus had... The way his theories have been abused, you kind of wish his mum had taken a baseball bat to him and got him a job as a milkman.

OLIVER
Cromwell

Oliver practices his Vinny Jones stare

any people believe that Oliver Cromwell is responsible for the establishment of parlia-mentary democracy. Others think he was a complete bastard who massacred lots of Irish people. I'd have had more respect for him if he hadn't had the same haircut as Cindy Crawford.

Oliver C was born in Huntingdon, where our own great John Major has his constituency, but there aren't many similarities between Major and Cromwell. Major looks like he couldn't punch his way out of a paper bag. If he had to fight our Queen in a civil war, I reckon she could floor him with a swift left hook to the upper lip (which he hasn't got) or a kick in the balls

Jo Brand – A Load of Old Balls

(which he hasn't got either).

Cromwell started off life as a gentleman farmer, which basically means he got lots of poor people to do the farming for him while he put his feet up. He served in parliament for a couple of years until King Charles I dissolved it. This was because in those days the King could do what he damn well wanted. Several years later the King said, 'I fancy another parliament,' and got it together again. Parliament tried to get the King to promise he wouldn't dissolve it again. But come on chaps, the King's the King…and he was no more likely to agree to that than to agree to having his head chopped off. (Ho! Ho! big surprise round the corner.) When the King refused to give his assurance that he wouldn't behave like a big baby, war between his lot and Ollie's lot broke out. This wasn't your poncey shouting rude names at each other at Prime Minister's Question Time but your full-scale charging-around-on-horse-back-and-killing-people type of war.

Cromwell and his mates had a couple of stunning victories, despite the fact that they didn't have Weetabix in those days, and Charles was taken prisoner. The problem was that the parliamentary side couldn't agree about anything except that they should fight Charles, probably because he looked a total wazzock, what with his Shirley Temple wigs and his silly shoes with big buckles on them. While they were bickering, Charles escaped (Group 4 obviously on security, then). War broke out again and this time Charles didn't get off so lightly: he had his head chopped off. Well, that's one way of stopping him wearing those dreadful wigs.

Because there was no telly in those days, about the only entertainment people got was the odd execution, which wouldn't go amiss in some of our more tedious soap operas. It would make a great game show, don't you think?

England then became

a republic but Cromwell still had enemies. Charles's son and supporters were agitating in Ireland and Scotland and Cromwell decided he had to sort them out once and for all. This he did in a big way. He systematically massacred a third of the Irish population. He wasn't discriminating either. His soldiers butchered women and children too. Oh, how marvellous to see a man of God at work. Thank goodness Cromwell wasn't an atheist or it could have been so much worse.

Cromwell was in trouble, though, because he hadn't paid his soldiers and also owed a lot of money to the blokes who had backed the war. To reward the soldiers and pay off his supporters all Roman Catholic landowners in Ulster, Leinster and

Royalists were gutted when Cromwell seized power

Jo Brand – A Load of Old Balls

Munster were ordered to leave their homes and migrate to Connaught or be shot. I don't think many of them said, 'Ooh, I'd like to be shot, please!' This incident led to the phrase 'To hell or Connaught'. So if an Irishman says this to you, you'll know what he's talking about and you'd better buy him a drink. I like to think of Cromwell as the Dame Shirley Porter of his age although, of course, Dame Shirley hasn't massacred anyone...yet.

So what was the matter with Oliver Cromwell?

First of all he was a Puritan, and Puritans were not the fun-loving, orgy-going, rubber-wearing mob that today's Tory Party are. The Puritans didn't like anything. They hated sex, gambling, drinking, dancing, games – anything that you might consider doing to enjoy yourself. This sort of attitude is always a bit suspect in the 'methinks they do protest too much' department. You always find that someone who loudly opposes something secretly loves it. That's why so many randy vicars end up running away with the Cub Mistress for a bit of dib dib dib. Oliver Cromwell probably fell into this category although, because *The News of the World* didn't exist at the time, no one rooted around and dug up any juicy scandal about him. I'm a bit pissed off about this because I would like to have been proved right.

Despite trying to be seen as a Christian bloke who just wanted democracy, Cromwell was in fact a military dictator. He was offered the throne of England more times than I've had hot dinners (if you believe that, you'll believe anything) but always refused. This is because he wasn't daft. He didn't want to

228

separate his head from his body as he'd just got a nice new hat for his birthday. Unfortunately, after he died he didn't have any choice about this: his body was dug up and his head stuck on a pole. Does the sophistication of the seventeenth century know no bounds? Well, my sophistication knows no bounds either. Cromwell was known as The Lord Protector. I prefer to think of him as The Big Durex.

There wasn't a Weightwatchers for horses in Cromwell's day

MICHELANGELO
Buonarroti

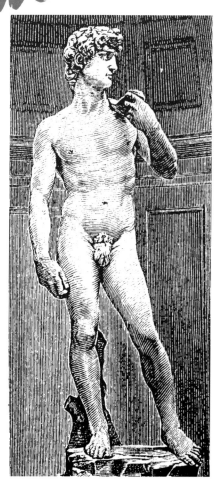

Nice legs, shame about the packet

'This *is* my cheerful face'

ichelangelo Buonarroti was born in 1475 in Caprese, Italy, and was not, as he sounds, a striker for AC Milan, but an artist.

His mother died when he was six and his father remarried.

At the age of thirteen Michelangelo was offered an apprenticeship to another artist called Ghirlandaio. His father wasn't keen because he thought his son was too good to be a painter. Perhaps he misunderstood and thought Michelangelo was going to end up putting an undercoat of eggshell white on the Pope's outside lav.

Michelangelo was always more interested in sculpture, because he reckoned he had 'sucked it from mother's milk in the marble quarry'. This is because in the old days people weren't quite so happy about women breast feeding in public and made them go to a local marble quarry to do it.

At the age of 15 Michelangelo was taken to live in the Medici Palace by Lorenzo the Magnificent – a very different approach from the present day. I can hardly see Her Majesty

'I half expected to find a replica of the *Pietà* with a little button you could press to hear the Virgin Mary saying "You should have had three Shredded Wheat"'

trawling through the students of St Martin's School of Art to find someone to go and live at Buckingham Palace and do a few nice corgi murals. But that was the way they did it then.

Most of Michelangelo's work consisted of commissions from Popes and posh people to do paintings for them. In those days, before they had cameras, lots of people wanted their portrait painted and, if Michelangelo was in a bad mood, he would paint very blurry pictures just like holiday snaps.

His first carving was entitled *The Rape of Dejanira*. In those days rape was considered a good subject for art.

Michelangelo was an all-round, good-at-everything type. Makes you sick, doesn't it? He was good at painting, good at sculpture, good at architecture and he still found time to write a few poems. Bet he couldn't pat his head and massage his tummy at the same time, though.

In 1496 he went to Rome to find a patron. This is because the Medicis didn't offer jobs for life in the same way the Tories can't guarantee them.

Michelangelo did quite well and got various commissions like the *Pietà* from a French Cardinal. The *Pietà* is a statue of the Virgin Mary holding the body of Christ in her arms. Unfortunately some years ago someone set about it with a hammer and it now has to be viewed behind a security screen.

'It is described in the Encyclopaedia Britannica as a sculpture of David, waiting quietly for Goliath. Can a statue wait any other way?'

Well, you'd think there were more worthy targets to set about with a hammer, like Eurodisney or a crispbread factory. The *Pietà* can be seen in St Peter's in Rome. I think it is a superb sculpture but unfortunately you can't view it without running the gauntlet of Roman souvenir shops which have the most tasteless souvenirs ever. Pictures of Jesus on the cross whose eyes follow you as you walk past, for example. I half expected to find a replica of the *Pietà* with a little button you could press to hear the Virgin Mary saying, 'You should have had three Shredded Wheat.'

After Michelangelo had finished the *Pietà* he couldn't get any more work in Rome and returned to Florence, where he was commissioned to do a statue of David for the cathedral building department. This took three years. Then a panel of great artists got together to discuss where it should go and eventually decided, very imaginatively, to put it in the Town Hall. It is described in the Encyclopedia Britannica as a sculpture of David, waiting quietly for Goliath. Can a statue wait any other way? Many critics believe the perspective is all wrong, but it has very small genitals, so I disagree with them on that score.

Michelangelo did a lot of work for Pope Julius II, including his tomb, which he never finished. Poor old Pope Julius couldn't wait and died anyway. Pope Julius also asked him to paint the ceiling of the Sistine Chapel. Originally the ceiling had stars on a blue background, so obviously the Pope was fed up with the Chapel looking like some crusty old hippy's bedroom.

The central portion of the ceiling was supposed to portray the twelve apostles and some grotesques, but Garry Bushell and Vinny Jones were unavailable to model for the grotesques, so this was replaced by prophets and sibyls and biblical histories. (Yawn.)

235

'Oh God, it looks like Giant Haystacks'

Many people think that in the scene depicting God creating Adam some lightning is flashing between God and Adam. This is because they have been watching the South Bank Show.

The Sistine Chapel took Michelangelo four years to complete. Some people find it hard to imagine spending four years on their back. However, any woman who has slept with a bloke who fancies himself as a bit of a stallion will known exactly what this is like.

The Sistine Chapel ceiling is absolutely stunning. Well, it would be, if you could see it without the accompaniment of hundreds of irritating schoolchildren who have about as much interest in it as I have in a career in synchronised swimming.

Michelangelo lived to be quite an old man, but in the last twenty-two years of his life he finished no sculpture, nor painting in the last fourteen. Still he was quite an old codger at this stage, so I think he can be forgiven. Besides older Italian men are too busy slavering over fat British women in their thirties. Well, that's certainly my experience.

IVAN
The Terrible

Ivan was so horrible he even tried to impale bees on his hat

*On important state occasions, Ivan always
held a swiss roll in his left hand*

Everyone has heard of Ivan the Terrible but few know why he was so terrible. Well, just to put the record straight, Ivan was a sadistic, hypocritical, vain, cold old bastard. And that was on his good days.

Ivan's dad, Vasily, the ruler of Muscovy, was quite a nice bloke until he realised his wife wasn't going to give him an heir. In those days infertility treatment was called 'being forcibly sent to a monastery while your old man tried another womb'. So Ivan's dad touted around for a new model and found a woman called Elena Glinskaya. Tragically she was fertile and in

Jo Brand – A Load of Old Balls

1530 out popped Ivan. It would have saved a lot of trouble if all Vasily's wives had had faulty apparatus.

Vasily died when Ivan was very young. He developed an infected abscess on his stomach which became very smelly and apparently it was quite difficult to be in the same room as he was. Legend has it that, when he died, the smell of the abscess turned into sweet perfume. Had this happened today, someone would have capitalised on it and produced Eau de Vasily's Rotting Entrails. The nearest we've got to it is Lily of the Valley.

'His favourite game was tearing feathers from birds, putting their eyes out and slitting their stomachs with a knife (Thank God for Lego)'

Ivan's mother was put in charge of running things but there was lots of plotting among the boyars (lads at court) to try to get the upper hand. Elena started her own mini reign of terror, executed a few people but eventually died herself, some say from poison. No one knows whether she smelt of Poison when she died. (This is a perfume I was given for my birthday and use as fly spray. It doesn't kill the flies but at least they smell nice.)

At this point Ivan was eight years old and already displaying symptoms of disturbance. His favourite game was tearing feathers from birds, putting their eyes out and slitting their stomachs with a knife. (Thank God for Lego.) He also liked hurling puppies from the ramparts of the palace, particularly when they had nicked all the toilet roll.

Ivan reckoned he became cruel because of his treatment at the hands of the boyars and he mentions an incident when one of the boyars ignored him and his brothers when they were playing. He was also outraged by the fact that sometimes he wasn't served his meals on time. Well, I've heard some excuses for criminal behaviour in later life but not getting your dinner on time has got to be the most evil.

240

At the age of 13 Ivan had had enough of late dinners and being ignored, so he invited the boyars to a feast and announced that he was taking over. He demanded that the ringleader of the trouble makers be put to death to demonstrate that the others supported him. This man was duly thrown into the street and devoured by hunting dogs. This may have taken some time as the dogs were all on crutches having been chucked off the ramparts as puppies.

By now Ivan was getting into his stride as a complete monster. He would go on hunting expeditions where it was par for the course to raid a village, steal all the food and rape the village girls. Respect for women in Russia at that time was zilch. They were considered the chief emissary of the devil. So handy to have an excuse to treat a whole sex like shit, isn't it? Thankfully we are not considered the chief emissary of the devil today, just assistant emissaries.

Tragically for the women of Russia, Ivan decided he wanted to marry when he was 17, so his staff were sent out all over the place to find suitable partners. It was a sort of Miss World competition – they were lined up in front of him and he chose the one he liked best. Unfortunately the prize wasn't travelling the world for a year; it was being married to Ivan the Puppy Murderer.

Ivan chose a woman called Anastasia who was very beautiful and very pious. (Two reasons to hate her, then.) So it wasn't what you'd call the perfect marriage. It was a bit like Jack Nicholson getting married to Mother Theresa. (Which may happen since he seems to be working his way through all the other women in the world.)

'It was a bit like Jack Nicholson getting married to Mother Theresa. (Which may happen since he seems to be working his way through all the other women in the world)'

241

'the men hurried home pretty sharpish to put Savlon on their heads and insure their beards for third party, fire and theft'

As an adult Ivan retained his sulky demeanour and childish temper. Once, while he was on holiday, a delegation came from a town called Pskov to complain about their governor. Ivan was furious at being disturbed, poured boiling alcohol over them and set fire to their beards. He ordered them to strip naked and was just about to do something *really* horrible, when news came that the great bell in the Kremlin had fallen. Ivan thought this was a sign from God, so he let the delegation go. I don't know if this is where the phrase 'saved by the bell' comes from but I bet the men hurried home pretty sharpish to put Savlon on their heads and insure their beards for third party, fire and theft.

Russian peasants were very superstitious. When fires destroyed Moscow they thought it was because a Moscow woman, Anna Glinsky, had torn out the hearts of corpses and sprinkled diabolical liquid all over the streets. Imaginative idea but a bit impractical. It's more likely it was caused by someone's beard after a visit to Ivan. They all rioted anyway.

Up until this point Ivan had always thought that God was his best mate, but the riots changed his mind and made him realise that perhaps God wasn't too pleased with his behaviour. Ivan decided he would become a goody-goody and started worrying about the morality of the people. (Bloody cheek.) He reorganised the country and brought in new laws.

Ivan still wanted a fight, though, and he decided to concentrate on the Tartars, wild tribesmen who were engaged in various skirmishes on the Russian borders. It was Christians versus Mohammedans again, just so you don't think he was free of religious bigotry. He besieged the town of Kazan and returned triumphant to Moscow. All was going well until Ivan got pneumonia and he declared that, if God spared him, he would go on a long pilgrimage. God did spare him, so off he went with his wife and son. His son died on the way, proving that you can't always trust God to do what you want. His wife had another son a year later but then died of a fever. Ivan would have been heartbroken if he'd had a heart, but instead he just went even more mad.

After 13 years of relatively wise government, with a wife who had curbed some of his worst excesses, he became a drunken monster. People were starting to call him Ivan the Terrible (not to his face, though, because he was too scary). Eventually he was betrayed by some of the boyars. One, Andre Kurbsky, went over to his enemy the King of Poland. He sent a messenger to Ivan to justify his actions. Ivan, not happy with the letter, drove the iron point of his staff through the messenger's foot, nailed it to the ground and leaned on it. Outrageous behaviour, much as we'd like to do this to the postman on gas-bill day. Ivan tortured the messenger for good measure and he and Kurbsky started a 15-year correspondence of hate. The messengers were obviously not happy about this. It was worse than trying to deliver to a house with a Rottweiler.

Ivan had married again by this time. His new wife was illiterate, spiteful and uncouth, so they were much better matched. Just when everyone was least expecting it, Ivan buggered off with his family, not leaving a forwarding address (to the relief of the messengers), and gave up the throne. A delegation of

'People were starting to call him Ivan the Terrible (not to his face though, because he was too scary)'

Church members and boyars caught up with him and begged him tearfully to come back (completely bloody barking the lot of them). Ivan agreed, provided the Church would let him do what he wanted. They agreed and shot themselves squarely in the foot as he eventually tortured most of them to death.

Jo Brand – A Load of Old Balls

Ivan employed a gang of thugs called the Oprichniki. These gangs were a bit like the secret police and enjoyed themselves torturing and murdering people all over the country. Sort of Guardian Angels with attitude. Despite this, the Russian people loved Ivan. But, as we've already heard, they believed fires were caused by diabolical liquid, so it's obvious they weren't the full kopek.

Ivan spent the rest of his life being horrible. He would massacre entire cities without so much as a touch of indigestion. His son was like him and they would divide their day between church and torture. How can you divide it? To me church is torture. Ivan married eight times and, after a big row with his son, struck out at him and killed him. (At one point he also tried to marry Elizabeth I of England. She had one brain cell, though, and steered well clear.) Ivan died on the exact date predicted by soothsayers. Pity they didn't predict what a nightmare he was going to be and drop him off the ramparts instead of a puppy.

After a night on the piss Ivan looked terrible

244

JACK
Charlton

'You're right Jack, that Nobby Stiles has got two
more hairs than what I have'

'I got that FIFA bloke right in the goolies'

ack Charlton would be made King of Ireland if there was such a position going. As it is, he knows that he has the adoration of a whole nation, which is a bit more than we can say for a certain Mr Graham Taylor who is several steps below a skunk wearing Impulse on the popularity ladder.

King Jack reckons he had no option about going into football. He came from a football oriented family; his mother was a cousin of Jackie Milburn and all her four brothers were professional footballers. Personally I'd like to have seen him have a crack at ballet, I'd love to have seen big Jack in *Swan Lake* sticking two fingers up at his family and head-butting Dame Margot.

Jack was always overshadowed a bit by brother Bobby, who everyone said would become a very good footballer. Jack meanwhile was a beanpole and a bit gangly. However, if Jack and Bobby were the last two men left on the earth, I know which one I'd go for and it wouldn't be little Bobby. Still, if there ever were only two blokes left on earth, knowing my luck they'd be Garry Bushell and Derek Beackon.

Enough of this girlie musing; back to Jack.

'Personally I'd like to have seen him have a crack at ballet, I'd love to have seen big Jack in *Swan Lake* sticking two fingers up at his family and head-butting Dame Margot'

At 15 Jack started work down the mine. His job title was 'hanger on and knocker off'. It had nothing to do with granting sexual favours to bored miners but, from what I can make out, involved pushing a load of coal round a corner. Jack, understandably, wasn't impressed and went to see the manager. After ascertaining that his job was going to be as dull as being support at a Bryan Adam's gig he resigned, which wound the manager up a treat as they'd just spent weeks training him.

Next Jack applied to be a policeman, for which it's essential to be good at kicking balls. He, never got the opportunity to pound the beat, though, because he was offered a trial for Leeds.

They offered him a job as a ground-staff boy. This is quite a good system where clubs get football-obsessed young boys to weed the grass and clean the bogs out, with the carrot of a possible substitute's place in the fifth team some seven years in the future. Then they sack them at their leisure.

At 17 Jack was signed by Leeds. He played one game and then had to go into the army. He was posted to the Guards at

'I know this bloody hat looks ridiculous'

Windsor, became captain of the football team and had a right cushy time by all accounts, getting himself ready for the real rumble back at Leeds.

The team Jack returned to at Leeds is described by him as, 'a bit iffy'. (This is a professional footballing term that I, as a girl, do not understand.) So Jack just mucked about, kicking the ball when it came his way, until a new manager, Don Revie, turned up. He really took an interest in Jack and said to him, 'If you were to screw the nut and do the job right, you could play for England.' Don and Jack spoke the same language. No one else could understand it, though.

Bobby Charlton, by this stage, was playing for Man Utd and their mum would say to Jack, 'Leave the littl'un alone'. This was not a hint that he should keep his hands out of his trouser pockets, but because Bobby was quite small.

Apparently there wasn't much rivalry between Jack and Bobby but one day Bobby put the ball through Jack's legs and Jack ran after him shouting, 'I'll get you, you little prat.' Thankfully their mum ran on to the pitch waving her handbag and broke things up.

When Bobby got picked to play for England, Jack was really pleased for him and didn't say this through gritted teeth at all.

Thankfully Jack was also picked to play for England and

relates that he had a good relationship with the goalkeeper Gordon Banks: 'We sorted that out after he punched me in the head a few times.' Nice to see that men can behave like adults about these things.

Of course our great moment of glory was in 1966, when England won the World Cup, and we have to cling tearfully on to that, because it doesn't look like we're going to win it again

'In his spare time he enjoys nothing better than standing up to his nuts in a raging torrent with a fishing rod in one hand and a bowl of Shredded Wheat in the other'

until Maradona stops sniffing a lot. When Geoff Hurst scored the winning goal Jack ran up the whole length of the pitch to grab him, but couldn't catch him because he was running in the opposite direction. Jack dropped to his knees and looked like he was praying. Of course some git took a photo and tried to pretend it was a great moment when in fact Jack was just knackered and trying to catch a fly that was annoying him.

Jack has gone from strength to strength and was made manager of the Ireland team in 1986. Since his discovery that Ireland could be represented by anyone who had a grandparent born there, the whole of Liverpool and the New York City Police Force have been queueing up to play.

In the 1994 World Cup Jack's team thrashed the Italians and looked like they were going places, while Jack charged up and down the edge of the pitch shouting at anyone who looked vaguely American, which is a good approach to have.

Jack is bolshy but he is a good laugh, not a particularly common characteristic in football managers. The Irish love him and it's probably the first time they haven't identified an Englishman with Oliver Cromwell.

Jack also has lots of hobbies. In his spare time he enjoys nothing better than standing up to his nuts in a raging torrent with a fishing rod in one hand and a bowl of Shredded Wheat in the other.

BONNIE PRINCE

Charlie

*Bonnie Prince Charlie persuaded many young women to
go into hand modelling*

Reading 'Big Sporran Wearers Weekly'

onnie Prince Charlie was always going to struggle with a name like Bonnie, but he was called The Young Pretender, so perhaps it wasn't his real name.

He was born in Rome in 1720, the son of James VIII, who was the King in exile of England and Scotland. His mother was Clementina, whom his father had married after he had looked for a wife all round Europe, with the requirements that she should be 'fit for childbearing', 'not ugly' and not have 'stinking breath'. Not setting his standards very high there, was he? I could have got that job. (Well, I clean my teeth.)

Jo Brand – A Load of Old Balls

As a child Charles had difficulty learning how to walk because he had weak knees – unlike his namesake Bonnie Langford, of course, who has very strong knees. Bonnie PC was fairly bright, however, and by the age of six spoke English, French and Italian, which is pretty impressive. English kids of that age now can't even manage English. Bonnie PC was brought up in Rome, which gave him something of a romantic view of the world. Little did he know that at some point his father would expect him to go back to England and claim the throne from the house of Hanover, which was Protestant. His father had had a couple of bashes but they weren't very successful, either because of bad weather or because he was feeling peaky or because, to be truthful, he was a bit wet and hopeless at fighting.

'he was probably some fat old git with no teeth and a dirty vest on'

Bonnie PC's dad worried about his son because he was a bit childish and tended to be into boy's stuff, so he eventually sent him on a tour of principal Italian cities to wise him up a bit. I can't really see the point of that. It hasn't suddenly made Gazza start quoting TS Eliot, has it? As he got older his dad was more and more keen for him to conquer England. The problem with this was lack of dosh and armies. As luck would have it a war between England and Spain gave Louis XV of France the idea that Bonnie PC could help him out: it seemed sensible to him to get someone else to do a bit of fighting. He had to find out how popular Bonnie was, so he sent a spy to England to find out. This spy was the sort who blabs at the first sight of pliers and shot his mouth off about his mission to anyone who would listen. Louis decided to invade anyway.

The king of England at the time was George I, who was hated because he was German, which has always been seen as a perfectly good reason to hate people. At least George and his advisors hated all the English too. One advisor said all

254

English women were ugly. But then again he was probably some fat old git with no teeth and a dirty vest on, so who cares?

Bonnie PC became a focus for rebellious Scots, a fiery people whose unquenchable spirit is shown by the fact that, despite all that has happened over the years, they still courageously insist on entering the World Cup. He finally got to Scotland by sneaking out of Rome and through France by pretending to go hunting. This clever scheme was worked out by his dad. Bonnie PC set off across the Channel disguised as a divinity student with a big hood over his crown, and a couple of choirboys in his suitcase, and the ship landed eventually off the Outer Hebrides. The Highland chiefs were a bit hesitant about whether to support Bonnie but in the end they decided it was a good way to keep warm.

'They had 8ft-long sticks with a scythe attached to the end of them and shouted quite a lot'

Bonnie PC's army took Edinburgh quite easily. I reckon this was because the Highlanders looked quite scary. They had 8ft-long sticks with a scythe attached to the end of them and shouted quite a lot. They stuffed the English army at Prestonpans, then headed towards England. The Highlanders apparently kept 'molesting' the baker's cart – perfectly understandable if he had some decent cakes. But they also broke into people's homes and nicked stuff. They laid siege to Carlisle, which surrendered, marched onwards past Manchester and got as far as Derby. English royalty, meanwhile, were taking it all very seriously. The Prince of Wales, celebrating the birth of his son, had a sugar fortress of Carlisle made and he and his mates threw sugar plums at it. What a stunning understanding of the political ramifications of the situation. Bonnie PC wanted to go all the way to London because he'd heard the Hamley's there was brilliant. The generals were not

255

so sure and really pissed him off by persuading him to retreat back to Scotland.

Bonnie PC's army had been doing very well until Culloden. Here he made a big mistake. His soldiers were knackered. They'd had only one biscuit that day. The baker said it was because they'd all raided his cart earlier. Bonnie PC decided to march to meet the Duke of Cumberland, whose army was well fed with sausage. They got

'Nice nails dear, but your thumbs are a bit stubby'

the timing wrong and arrived too late, so had to leg it back. Bonnie PC thought he was invincible, so he stayed to fight and his army was routed. Sadly, once when I was doing a gig in Glasgow suffering from very bad PMT, I reminded the audience of the English performance at Culloden. Strangely it didn't go down too well.

Bonnie PC fled, as princes are very conveniently allowed to do. It's easy for them because they always stand at the back of a battle so they have more of a chance of getting away. Bonnie escaped to Skye with the help of Flora McDonald, who disguised him as a maid, Betty Burke. People were suspicious of this maid who was very tall and hopeless at manipulating her petticoats. Nobody sussed it, though, because all the Scots

256

wore some sort of skirt at the time.

Flora was captured soon after and imprisoned in the Tower. She became a celeb and her descendants went on to form the McNugget clan. The Duke of Cumberland's men went on the rampage, looting, pillaging and being as revolting as most men can be, given the chance. Bonnie PC returned to France, where he had numerous ridiculous affairs and was eventually forced to go into hiding.

He thought up various stupid schemes to regain power: in one he went to England disguised as a monk with an eye-patch. What a master of disguise. Finally he married a 19-year-old. She was described as attractive and mischievous, he as corpulent, crippled and spotty. He drank so much he couldn't control his bowels. She left him. I can't imagine why.

Bonnie PC had a stroke aged 67 and died three days later. No one wants to die a sad, embittered old drunkard but that's what happened and, with a name like Bonnie Prince Charlie, who would have thought it?

JOSEF
Stalin

Stalin's hair, eyebrows and moustache were in constant competition for that Harmony hairspray look

Stalin watching Countdown and planning to execute Richard Whitely

osef Stalin was born in poverty (a small town in Georgia) in 1879. He was called Dzhugashvili, but changed his name later to Stalin, which means 'Man of Steel'. What a modest chap he was, then.

Josef had a horrible dad who drank and talked cobblers – I mean, was a cobbler. Mr Dzhugashvili beat his son brutally but cheered him up by dying when Josef was 11. Judging by Stalin's record, however, the damage had already been done. He was so like his dad that his main relaxation was sitting down of a night with a shoe to mend, 14 pints of Special Brew and a kid to smack.

Stalin attended church school, where they did their bit to instil him with good Christian values. Or to put it another way,

> ## 'his main relaxation was sitting down of a night with a shoe to mend, 14 pints of Special Brew and a kid to smack'

they had about as much effect on him as The Flat Earth Society have on the Round The World Yacht Race.

Stalin was later expelled from a theological seminary for spreading subversive ideas. I shouldn't think in an institution as restrictive as a church seminary it's particularly difficult to have a subversive idea. Asking for Jaffa Cakes instead of Rich Tea biscuits would have been enough to get me drummed out of Sunday School, especially as the vicar in my local church was the Kentish village personification of Stalin. All right, he wasn't responsible for the scale of horror that Stalin was but he did throw croquet balls at his wife's ankles and make lots of kids cry. This gave me as much respect for the Church as I have for Mills & Boon's feminist ideals.

Back to Stalin, who at this point

Stalin hadn't quite got the hang of self-abuse

decided to get involved in the underground Marxist movement. As usual, this lot, who were supposed to be working for the good of the people, couldn't even agree among themselves and the party was split between the Mensheviks (moderates) and the Bolsheviks (big-style hard geezers). Stalin joined the Bolsheviks and very aptly too, because he turned out to be a right bolshy bastard. He was often imprisoned but escaped several times, leading to speculation that he was either a double agent or very good at escaping.

Stalin didn't do much to help in the revolution of 1917 but by 1922 he had become general secretary of the Communist Party and was famed throughout the land for his well-kept nails, shorthand speed and imagination at buying the boss's wife birthday presents. Lenin wasn't keen on Stalin and warned that he was too ruthless but Stalin's face had made the very clever move of looking friendly and avuncular and so, people being stupid, everyone thought that he was probably quite nice. After Lenin died Stalin managed to suppress all his warnings and joined forces with two other big-nob Communists to defeat Trotsky, whom Lenin had wished to succeed him. Trotsky was banished from Russia and later bumped off in Mexico, with an ice-pick in the study. Yes, apparently they did have Cluedo in Mexico.

Stalin then turned on his two allies and connived his way round all the other potential leaders until, in the early 30s, he became the sole leader of the Communist Party. Not content with this (and, let's face it, he could have had a pretty good life sipping borsch, eating turnips and swanning about the garden in a pair of black-market Levis), he instigated a series of political purges.

If you have a paranoid personality, you tend to think people are saying horrible things about you and you irritate your friends by saying things like 'You just said I was fat', when they've been talking about someone's cat. If you have a paranoid personality and you happen to be in charge of a massive country, however, you're not content with crossing people off your party list; you become a killing machine for anyone who gets in your way. People have only to do the tiniest thing to annoy you and they're as good as pushing up the daisies. Then, once you've killed all your rivals, you begin to think that perhaps

Stalin's hairdresser cleverly trained his moustache into the shape of a hat

the people that grassed them up aren't kosher either, so you have to bump them off too. In the end there's only you, a couple of old ladies and a hamster left in the entire country. This is what happened to Stalin. Anyone who didn't agree with him, criticised the party or laughed at his moustache had had it.

'Anyone who didn't agree with him, criticised the party or laughed at his moustache had had it'

Those people he didn't have killed he forced to work in collective farms, thereby starving millions of peasants to death. Anyone who pointed out that collective farming was as successful as an Al Jolson record at a Ku Klux Klan party disappeared as well.

'Learning lessons from history just seems to mean stuffing the enemy better the next time round'

Stalin was jealous that the rest of Europe was far ahead of Russia industrially, so he moved very quickly to remedy this. Historians agree, in an unemotional way, that he was fairly successful in this, but then again most historians are men with the social conscience of a wombat.

In 1939 Stalin made a non-aggression pact with Hitler. That's a laugh, the two biggest bastards in the world getting together to talk cooperation. It's like Michael Portillo and Peter Lilley getting together to discuss how they could improve the lives of single mothers.

Unsurprisingly the pact lasted about as long as Gazza's hanky stays dry and eventually they fought each other in the Second World War. Stalin, being on the winning side, managed to grab a bit more land for Communism to ravage and to starve all the inhabitants.

The Second World War was followed by the Cold War, during which Western Europe and Russia hissed at each other through the Iron Curtain.

Stalin died in 1953 and his body was preserved. Bet they needed a big jar for that. He is now

265

It was a big effort to look pissed off when Stalin snuffed it

abhorred as a tyrant, showing once again we shut the stable door about twenty years too late as far as cold-blooded murderers in history are concerned. Learning lessons from history just seems to mean stuffing the enemy better the next time round.

So what about Stalin's family life? Any clues there to explain his outrageous public behaviour? Stalin's first wife died of TB, he remarried but his second wife also snuffed it. The word is that either she committed suicide or he killed her. His son Jacob was captured by the Germans, who offered to exchange him, but Stalin turned the offer down and Josef died in a prison camp. Of his other children, his son became an alcoholic and his daughter defected to the US. It's not exactly *The Darling Buds Of May*, is it?

MICHAEL
Jackson

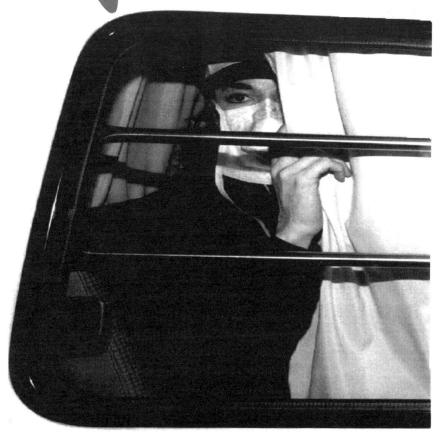

'Shall I have the grey backdrop for my passport photos?'

'Oh shit! Pants outside trousers again'

ittle Peter Pan Jackson was born in Gary, Indiana, and was the seventh of nine children, so the obvious choice was to become a singing group or a netball team. None of the brothers wanted to play goal defence, so a singing group it was.

Michael says his mother was great. She loved them a lot and taught them lots of things. His father, however, he says, 'built a shell around himself', which could have been a DIY experiment that went wrong. If the family were all together his father would leave the room, embarrassed. Not surprising, if he looked like a great big hermit crab.

Michael's experiences of clubs as a child were not particu-

Jo Brand – A Load of Old Balls

larly positive. The Jackson Five would work in Chicago in between a bad comedian and a stripper. (God, didn't they have social workers in America in the 60s?) The boys would amuse themselves by looking through a hole in the wall into the ladies' toilet, which Michael describes as 'really wild'. I think 'sad' is the word you're search for there, Michael.

One incident which really affected Michael as a child was seeing a transvestite at one of these clubs. Perhaps that's where LaToya got the idea from. As a child he spent lots of time at Diana Ross's house and apparently she taught him all she knew. Judging by her recent appearance in the '94 World Cup she didn't teach him anything about football. Michael describes Diana as his mother, lover and sister all combined in one person. Oo... er, missus, call the child psychiatrist pronto.

The Jackson Five would get up to high jinks on tour. There would be shaving cream fights, paper bags full of water, pillow fights. Not exactly rock and roll, is it? No tellies through the window, no groupies. Still I suppose he was only a nipper at the time.

One great source of anguish to Michael, which has stayed with him, was his skin. He had very bad acne which, he says, 'messed up my whole personality'. It would have needed to be like the Elephant Man's to get him into the state he seems to be in at the moment. Old Daddy-in-a-shell didn't help. He would bring a bunch of girls into the bedroom when Michael and Jermaine were asleep, and they would wake up to find these girls giggling. What sort of monster was this man? Not so much a dad, more a a weasel with an eye on the kid's wallet.

Michael's adolescence seems to have buggered him up for ever. He says the main problem was that he didn't look like a sweet little boy any more and people didn't recognise him. And if they didn't recognise him then, they certainly won't now. He

'I tell you my hair is sharp – look it's cut my fingers'

was gangly, tall and basically turning into a grown-up, which he didn't want to do. His records were selling in their millions all over the world and all he wanted was to be six again. The only reason I'd like to be six again is so I could have an Aztec bar.

At 21 Michael took stock of his life and decided he needed to get control. Out of all the people he had to take into consideration God was at the top of his list. God must have told him to do some firing because he started with his dad. Firing your dad can't be easy. I can't imagine it. Then again, I'm a comic and my dad's an expert on scaffolding,

271

Jo Brand – A Load of Old Balls

so I don't suppose a situation would arise where I had to employ him – not unless he was advising on the scaffolding I need to keep my leggings up.

'I am the loneliest person in the world,' says Michael. He hasn't met anyone that works in a lighthouse then. The problem with Michael Jackson is he's never done anything normal. His first real date was with Tatum O'Neal, for God's sake. On this date they went to a party at Hugh Hefner's playboy mansion. It's hardly the pictures and a quick grope behind the kebab house, is it? He also fell in love with Tatum and calls her his first love after Diana. He says he was hurt and jealous when Diana got married. He's also dated Brook Shields and says Liza Minelli is a good friend.

Musically people think he's brilliant. I have to say it's not my cup of tea. I was quite happy with the Jackson Five but, when we got all this crotch-grabbing, white-gloves nonsense, I thought the lad had lost it. Before our very eyes he has turned into a junior Phantom of the Opera. Michael denies he had anything done apart from a nose job and a cleft in his chin. And now he's in deep trouble over possible child abuse. He's out of his bonce on painkillers, his best friend is a chimp, he's got a funfair in his garden, and the best fun he's had in the last ten years is wearing a surgical mask the dentist gave him. Not exactly an advert for stardom, is it? I don't think I'll write any more jokes. I think I'll go back to nursing.

Michael holds the piece of silicone he is about to have transplanted into his face

272

SIGMUND *Freud*

*Sigmund wonders how to operate the
'What the butler saw' machine*

*Sigmund never wore any other mac
to the GoGo Dolly Club in Vienna*

igmund Freud has me down as a neurotic, stuck in the oral phase of development. This is because I eat, smoke and suck my thumb. I have him down as a tight-arsed pervy stuck in the knob mag stage of development.

Freud has had a tremendous influence on our emotional lives and the psychiatric profession swallowed him hook, line and sinker for a long time. How very oral of them! His life story isn't particularly fascinating. Born in what is now the Czech Republic, he went to Vienna when he was four and as an adult

Jo Brand – A Load of Old Balls

worked there in the medical profession. He produced a series of papers and books in which he attempted to explain the working of the unconscious mind. For those who slept through school, this doesn't mean the mind of someone who has been knocked out. It means the working of our brains about which we are unaware, which is roughly 97 per cent of mental activity in the case of rugby players... and that's being generous.

'The one pretending to be "Bulldog Drummond" is definitely vice squad'

Freud suggested that the mind was made up of three bits, the id, the ego and the super-ego: the id being the instinctive wild bit of our mind, the ego the conscious bit that makes decisions and the superego the internalised adult side of the brain that controls the other two. Think of them as three characters: the id is like Shane McGowan, the ego like Tony Blair and the superego like Judge Pickles. So your brain is a constant battle between Id McGowan wanting to get pissed and out of it, Judge Superego threatening to hang you if you do and Ego Blair in the middle saying, 'Oh come on, it's all right to have a little drink.' No wonder loads of us go doolally.

Freud always claimed his work was scientific but he never went anywhere near a Bunsen burner and all his subjects were young, middle-class women suffering from some form of hysteria... an expense account of Princess Dianas, to use the collective noun.

Freud had some weird ideas. My favourite is penis envy. He thought us girls were jealous of the penis. Don't be ridiculous, Sigmund. Who wants an elongated mushroom ruining the line of their leggings? The only time I am envious of the penis is when it comes to having a pee in uninviting circumstances, like on the top deck of the bus at 2am. The Tory government's new anti-squatting laws are going to make this even more difficult.

'The only time I am envious of the penis is when it comes to having a pee in uninviting circumstances, like on the top deck of the bus at 2am'

Many of Freud's concepts were lifted from Greek mythology and one thing has always puzzled me about this – what sort of theories would he have produced if the Greeks hadn't been so keen on a good story of sex and violence? never been written? In the legend of Oedipus, for instance, our eponymous (flash word or what?) hero kills his dad, marries his mum and then blinds himself when he realises what he's done. That's not fodder for a serious scientist, that's a bleeding Brookside script.

I think it would have been far more interesting if Freud had based his theories on stories like Little Red Riding Hood, which demonstrates that all girls are nice and helpful and all blokes are wolves who just want to eat us. Would have been a lot more accurate too.

Freud's work has been taken most seriously by the Americans, all of whom are deeply committed to analysis. This is because analysis allows you to talk non-stop about yourself for periods of up to an hour. Can you think of anything more tedious? The only way therapists avoid going off their heads is by charging people money to do this. It's very reassuring to see how successful therapy can be – look at Woody Allen, for example, who has had thousands of hours of analysis and still behaves like a knob-brain, getting off with a girl half his age and calling his child Satchel. Warms the cockles of your heart, doesn't it?

Freud is best known for his Freudian slip which apparently

Jo Brand – A Load of Old Balls

isn't a piece of underwear but a demonstration of the unconscious mind at work. This is when you mean to say something and a totally unexpected word pops out. So, for example, you might *mean* to say, 'I'd like a salad', but what you actually come out with is 'I'd like three Big Macs, fries and twelve cherry pies'. So that's always very handy.

Lots of academics can't agree on Freud and an argument is currently raging between them about the value of his work. Still I suppose it gives them something to do apart from getting more crumbs in their beards and trying to get off with nubile students. In my work as a psychiatric nurse dealing with emergencies I saw a lot of poor people who were in a bad way because their analysis had been terminated or they couldn't afford to pay for it any more. Lots of Freudian analysts say it's important for their patients to pay because it strengthens the therapeutic relationship and sets up an appropriate contractual bond. Yeah, pull the other one: it's got balls, I mean bells, on!

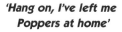

'Hang on, I've left me
Poppers at home'

278

NICCOLÒ
Machiavelli

*Machiavelli wore long dresses and stood on a plinth
to disguise his stubby little body*

*He came third in a Norman Tebbit
look-alike competition*

nyone interested in maintaining and increasing
his power should make use of deceitfulness and
cunning combined with the ruthless use of force'

Party political broadcast? Leeds United football manual? Estate agents' drinking song? Unfortunately not. These are the words of one Niccolò Machiavelli, an Italian civil servant and one of the few people in history to have his name made into a proper word. 'Machiavellian' is used to describe someone who operates in an underhand way. 'Brandian', which will hopefully come into the language one day, describes someone who can't get a husband but doesn't give a toss.

Machiavelli was a clever political strategist who pledged allegiance to whoever was in power; consequently nobody trusted him as far as they could throw him. As he was a bit pinched and skinny, however, this

'He was sent on many diplomatic missions, which is a bit like sending Mike Tyson to work at a Rape Crisis Centre'

was quite a long way. Machiavelli was quite open about how untrustworthy he was, describing himself as someone who 'has no respect for anyone in Italy, though he bows and scrapes to those better dressed than himself'. Glad I don't have to do that; I'd spend the whole bloody day bowing and scraping.

The jury is out on Machiavelli. Some people think he was a nasty piece of work while others think he told it like it was. I don't see why he can't be both. You don't have to be nice to tell the world what's going on, as tabloid reporters have proved time and time again. But then again they don't really tell the world what's going on either.

Machiavelli was born in Florence, to a reasonably well-off family. Florence was ruled by one of the Medicis, Lorenzo the Magnificent. (I bet he chose that name himself.) After Lorenzo died the Medicis were driven out of Florence and it became a republic. Machiavelli became a civil servant and worked for the republic for 14 years. He was sent on many diplomatic missions, which is a bit like sending Mike Tyson to work at a Rape Crisis Centre.

The republic didn't last, however, and those Medicis came back with a vengeance. Machiavelli was arrested under suspicion of plotting against them and was tortured. He would not change his story, though. I can't understand this. As soon as anyone came near my hands with a pair of pliers I'd even tell them where I'd hidden my emergency Snickers.

Eventually Machiavelli was released and he spent the next 15 years petitioning the Medicis for another job. But the

Medicis didn't trust him and, to stave off madness at the little estate where he lived, he would put on his courtly clothes every evening and hold imaginary conversations with some of the greatest statesmen in history about their motives and strategies. He wrote down these conversations and distilled their wisdom into *The Prince* or *Everything You Wanted To Know About Being A Despot But Were Too Thick To Ask.*

The main advice contained in the book is that a good prince should ignore moral considerations and have a good army. I've always had my suspicions about civil servants. A lot of them seem to be those weedy little blokes who look like they wouldn't hurt a fly and then turn out to be the local serial killer.

'The Prince sold well among despots and despot wannabes. William of Orange even slept with a copy under his pillow. Perhaps he thought the despot fairy would leave him a kingdom'

Machiavelli felt, as the leader of a state, that it was safer to be feared than loved. I can see his point. It's much more fun to scare someone into going out with you than have them phoning up all the bloody time and leaving soppy messages. Cynical? Me?

The Prince sold well among despots and despot wannabes. William of Orange even slept with a copy under his pillow. Perhaps he thought the despot fairy would leave him a kingdom.

Many academics have dismissed *The Prince* as a handbook for dictators but the current thinking is that Machiavelli was idealistic and patriotic. Perhaps *The Prince* was ghost-written for him by some local medieval psycho. There certainly were loads to choose from at the time: Cesare Borgia was doing an Open University course in torture and face rearranging and we know that Machiavelli was a big fan of his.

Jo Brand – A Load of Old Balls

Machiavelli thought it was perfectly all right to be ruthless but didn't agree with senseless cruelty. Well, that is big of you, mate. I suppose it hadn't occurred to you that all cruelty is senseless.

It's a pity someone didn't get Machiavelli in a room and sing him a few choruses of 'Where Have All The Flowers Gone?'. Then perhaps he and Cesare could have gone off on an *Iron John* type new man weekend in the forest and learnt how to cry. I could have helped with the learning how to cry bit.

Machiavelli was unpopular with the established Church, so there were some good things about him. Many churchmen thought of him as the antichrist and you can see why, because he does bear a passing resemblance to Norman Tebbitt.

So let's look at the evidence. Civil servant, fond of ruthlessness, admirer of the Borgia brigade, immune to torture, writer of early snuff movie scripts. Sounds quite a little sweetie, doesn't he?

Machiavelli said people never change, that each generation makes the same stupid mistakes as the previous one and therefore you can foretell future political events by studying the past. I see what he means. After the First World War thousands of people said: 'This must never happen again. Oh dear, it just has.'

Machiavelli should have been able to predict his own future by this method, because years later, when the Medicis were finally driven out, he gleefully applied for his old job back and was turned down because he'd been a little bit too friendly with the Medicis and was now considered untrustworthy. This came as such a shock to Machiavelli that the spirit drained out of him, he took to his bed and was dead within a week. All the imaginary figures round his bed must have been a bit pissed off that they didn't have anyone to talk to any more.

JOHN F
Kennedy

JFK wonders why Jackie is holding a miniature model of Patrick Moore

JFK liked applause so much he hired his own seal to stand at the back and clap during press conferences

hey say that everyone can remember where they were on the day that John F Kennedy got shot. Well, I can't. I was six at the time, so I was either at Brownies, in bed or tied to a tree somewhere being beaten up by my brothers who favoured the Machiavellian* school of play. John F Kennedy was descended from Irish immigrants who had left Ireland because of the potato famine and he had a middle-class upbringing in Boston – which means he probably never met Norm in Cheers. John was educated privately

*see page 278 for the low-down on this slimy bastard

and went on to Princeton where he was more interested in sport than in politics. So is Sebastian Coe but that hasn't stopped him weasling his way into the Tory Party and becoming an MP.

John F was in the Navy for a while and had a real *Boy's Own* adventure when the boat he was commander of sank and he and the other sailors had to swim to a small island, from which they were rescued a few days later. There is no record of the pieces of music he would have chosen for *Desert Island Discs* but, as he was discharged from the navy because of malaria, we can safely assume 'Feeling Hot, Hot, Hot' was probably in there. He entered the House of Representatives at the age of 29 but, as he was a dedicated womaniser, this is not surprising.

His love of 'how's your father' seems to have been inherited from his dad, Joseph, who pursued anything in a skirt. (Well, apart from Scotsmen and nuns.) John is quoted as saying, 'Dad told all the boys to get laid as often as possible.' Good old Dad. No words of wisdom about respect for women or the dangers of sexually transmitted disease then?

Most boys do the opposite of what their dads tell them but John was a good boy, so he launched into an orgy of copulating. While in the navy his nickname was 'Shafty', which tells us all we need to know about what a sensitive and caring lover he was. A reporter with whom he'd had an affair said, 'Sex to him was like a cup of coffee.' Well I drink about ten cups a day, so he must have been at it

J F Kennedy

*The groom does up his trousers after
paying the vicar the usual JFK way*

non-stop. He apparently tried to pull Marlene Dietrich in a lift but had the decency first to check with her whether she'd shagged his dad or not. What a gentleman!

But old Johnny-come-lately wanted to become president and too much nomping was frowned upon in a presidential candidate, so he needed somewhere to go and 'have coffee' without being rumbled. His friend, the actor Peter Lawford, provided this at his posh home which is where his infamous, yet unproven, affair with Marilyn Monroe was supposed to

289

have taken place. Marilyn says they did, Peter Lawford (when he's sober) says they didn't but apparently he told two of his wives (when he was drunk) that they did. So who knows? Marilyn always made sure she referred to him as the President in company and, judging by his attitude to women, he probably made her call him that when they were alone and in the sack as well.

> **'Most boys do the opposite of what their dads tell them but John was a good boy, so he launched into an orgy of copulating'**

I don't imagine JFK's womanising was to popular with his wife or, as he was Catholic with his priest for that matter. He married Jaqueline Lee Bouvier in 1953 and on the outside they appeared to be the perfect *Hello* couple, but this didn't seem to stop him nipping off to Pete's for the odd bunk-up. And it's not as if he was just an incurable romantic. (Yeah, we've all heard that excuse.) As soon as he'd seduced one woman he would get bored and move on to another. Even the 'sex goddess' Marilyn didn't escape this treatment but, by all accounts, she managed to stay in with the family, moving quickly on to brother Bobby. (Isn't it nice to see brothers sharing?) She never got round to Teddy as he was too busy driving through 20-foot deep puddles with his secretary and practising breaststroke.

JFK was well-loved as a President because he was handsome and charming. He also made great speeches. My favourite is the one he made in Germany, when he said, 'Ich bin ein Berliner.' This was supposed to mean, I am a Berliner, but in Germany a Berliner is a type of doughnut. The people of

> **'He apparently tried to pull Marlene Dietrich in a lift but had the decency first to check with her whether she'd shagged his dad or not'**

Germany must have been very impressed by his grasp of regional cakes.

Highlights of Kennedy's career included the Cuban crisis, when the filthy Commies (the American word for the Russians) started to install long-range missiles in Cuba. Kennedy faced up to them and Kruschev, the Russian leader, backed down. So the Commies weren't that filthy after all – not compared to smutty old JF anyway.

Kennedy was also responsible for kicking off the space programme which put a man on the moon. This was mighty impressive and an extraordinarily expensive way to improve a couple of astronauts' golf. Pity they didn't manage to follow it up with a McDonald's up there. On the other hand, the moon is the only place that the Americans have left alone once they'd got there. It's the only place you can get a bit of peace and quiet these days without someone in a loud shirt coming up and shouting at you.

So, John F Kennedy, famous for being assassinated, I'm afraid, but generally acknowledged as a good President and a great shag. People often wonder what the F stands for in JFK. I've told you he was a womaniser...use your imagination.

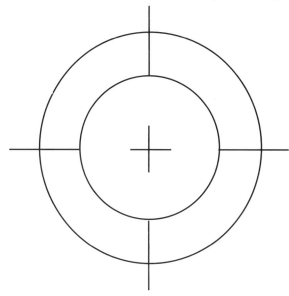

RABBIE
Burns

Rabbie was very good at the game of 'statues'

An attractive couple in love – Yuk!

abbie Burns was born in 1759. His father was a gardener and, as a child, Rabbie had relatives who told him lots of strange stories about kelpies, fairies and spunkies. This accounted for his love of legends and shagging women, I suppose. People were very superstitious in those days and a story from round the area at that time illustrates this. An old lady passing by a churchyard at night saw a creature with horns making a terrible bellowing noise and assumed it was the devil. What had actually happened was that one of the local farmer's bullocks (yes, *bullocks)* had got trapped in the church wall. So that shows how daft they were.

As a younger man Rabbie was bashful and awkward with

women but, as he grew up, he became quite a ladies' man. (Ladies' man is of course a euphemism for out and out penetrator *extraordinaire*.) I've noticed this before. Some young blokes, because they're a bit spotty and unattractive as adolescents, as soon as they throw off the yoke of acne and awkwardness have to impregnate the world. Others, of course, always looked all right and just love a bit of rumpy-pumpy anyway, but they're not so much fun because they aren't so grateful.

Burns formed the Bachelors Club with a few friends, two requirements of which were that you had to have a frank and honest heart and you must be a professed lover of one or more of the female

'The third requirement which wasn't mentioned was that you had to be an arsehole'

sex. The third requirement, which wasn't mentioned, was that you had to be an arsehole.

Robert was a flax-dresser for a while, whatever that is, and at this point he started to sow the wild oats big time. He seduced Betsy Paton, a female servant. She is described as plain looking, rude and uncultivated, and having a strong masculine understanding and contempt for every sort of refinement. Sounds great, doesn't she? The problem in those days was that, if you nomped someone, they invariably got pregnant. Nobody had heard of contraception and the blokes that had, like today, probably thought it was a bit sissy. Rabbie didn't feel obliged to marry but moved on to the next one, Jean Armour, whose cheek flamed scarlet and jet-black eyes sparkled dangerously. Sounds a bit mad to me.

After a year Jean found herself 'as women wish to be who love their lords'. It took me a long time to work out that this means pregnant as well. It would be great if you went to the doctor's to hear the results of a pregnancy test and the doctor said, 'You are as you'd wish to be if you love your lord.' I'd punch him in the gob.

Rabbie Burns

Rabbie was beginning to be a bit of a writer by this stage:
I am nae poet in a sense
But just a rhymer like by chance.
That doesn't even rhyme, Rabbie dear (or maybe it does if you're pissed).

Jean Armour's family were a bit odd and not a very open-minded lot. Her brother Adam and some of his mates had got a woman of loose morals and put her, with no knickers on, on a pine log and dragged it out of town attached to a horse so that her rude bits were severely lacerated. What

'I'd like to have got hold of him and dragged him by his goolies through a hedgehog colony'

charming fellows they must have been. This is the ultimate in double standards. He didn't mind that some crappy old local poet had got his sister up the duff but he couldn't abide prostitutes. I'd like to have got hold of him and dragged him by his goolies through a hedgehog colony. Then Rabbie could have written a nice poem about it.

Jean Armour actually rejected Rabbie, under pressure from her family. Her dad was very angry indeed and tried to get all his money off him. Seeing as he only had about ten pence and a couple of buttons, it hardly seems worth it. Jean Armour had twins. Rabbie remarked in poetry that women had been designed: 'to temper man, we had been brutes without you'. I dread to think what men would have been like if there were no women. I can hardly say they're sweet and lovely with us around.

While Jean was pregnant Robert had moved on to someone else. He had been thinking of going away to the West Indies to make his fortune. He had a ticket but couldn't make up his mind to go, so he went to Edinburgh instead, which is known as the Athens of the North.

297

Jo Brand – A Load of Old Balls

Burns discovers that Highland Mary has an interesting problem

Can't think why. There's no smog or men trying to put their hands up your skirt...unfortunately. Edinburgh in those days wasn't the posh snobby town it is today. It was 'a seething mass of females abandoned to crime and vice.' What a shame it's changed, although in my experience it is still like that during the Edinburgh Festival.

During his Edinburgh period Burns was becoming quite a popular poet. He went on four tours and was a bit like an early rock star. Although there were no tellies to throw out of the window or cocaine to snort, the drinking and copulating certainly lived up to expectations. He left a trail of expanding women in his wake.

One thing Burns suffered from was depression. Medicine in those days wasn't nearly as sophisticated as it is now and Burns thought he could sort himself out by taking laxatives. Of course these days, with modern technology, it's several thousand volts through your cranium. Think I'd rather go down the stewed prunes route.

Jean got pregnant again with twins following a visit from Rabbie. Her dad had had enough and turned her out of the house. Rabbie, meanwhile,was having an affair with someone called Agnes whom he had renamed Clarinda. Lucky old her. They sent letters to each other and swooned a lot and eventually Agnes went back to her husband in the West Indies only to find he had another woman. That's life, eh?

Rabbie got a job at the Excise, which involved travelling round the country trying to catch out people who were illegally brewing booze. This didn't quite fit with his Socialist stance but apparently he tried to be as nice as a snooping government employee can be. He eventually got together with Jean and set up as a farmer. He wasn't very good at it but he was still good at sowing because he got two more women pregnant. Jean laughed this off and said he should have had two wives. Perhaps he hadn't told her about the other five hundred women.

Burns is still a very popular poet today and particularly popular in Japan for some reason I don't understand. As with Shakespeare at school, a lot of his poems have been cleaned up for children's consumption. Given that he was such an all-round lusty, bawdy man I suppose it would be weird to assume his poems could all be flowery and sweet. If you don't believe me, get hold of a copy of his unabridged work, but don't show it to your parents.

Alphonse *Capone*

*Al turned to crime after Bob Hoskins
beat him to the lead in Roger Rabbit*

Al always tried to get at least one fat person to stand next to him to make him look thinner

A l Capone, or 'Scarface' as he was known, is perhaps the world's most famous gangster apart from Marlon Brando, or 'The Godfather' as he is known.

Al's family went to America from Italy, seeking their fortune. His dad, who was a qualified barber, had trouble finding work, so he made do with working in a grocery store until he got his own shop. In those days in Brooklyn barbers did lots of other things apart from cutting hair. They would also pull teeth and bleed people, which may be where little Alphonse got the idea of being a gangster.

As soon as he was old enough to commit crime, little Al

joined a gang called the South Brooklyn Rippers. Initially they weren't into serious crime but just went round causing a bit of mayhem as teenage delinquents love to do. It was very important to be in a gang in those days because it gave you a sense of identity and killing and torturing people is always so much more fun if you're with your mates.

At the age of 19 Al met an Irish girl called Mae at a dance and fell in love. They married but didn't stay together for

Al's wife often got hungry and tried to eat her coat

too long because at this point Al was hanging around with bigger boys causing more trouble. After a fight he was sent by his gang boss to Chicago for his own safety.

The song 'My Kinda Town Chicago Is' was made for Al Capone. The town and the man were both corrupt and crime-ridden. Al began to think seriously about his future as a gangster and, when prohibition began, he realised there was a lot of money to be made. If there's one thing we all love it's getting pissed.

'It was very important to be in a gang in those days because it gave you a sense of identity and killing and torturing people is always so much more fun if you're with your mates'

Bootlegging became a full-time occupation. By this I mean supplying alcohol illegally, not taping a Morrisey gig from 200 yards away using a crappy old tape recorder and then trying to sell it down the market.

'Capone built a big brothel at Forest View. It had huge windows looking out on to the town, so the locals used to say "Big brothel is watching you"'

Capone's boss was a man called Torrio and his gang was un-rivalled in Chicago. Torrio felt safe enough to take his parents back to Italy, where he had bought them a huge villa with 15 servants. They weren't used to this and left most of the servants in the cupboard all day.

Torrio had left Al in charge and he did very well, expanding 'the business'. The business consisted of gambling and protection rackets, the occasional brothel and a fair bit of beating, torture and killing. It was grown-up little boys with real guns who didn't have to listen to their mums any more.

Capones gang even took over a village called Forest View, which had been built by war veterans. (Pity they didn't build any bunkers round it.) When the founder of the village raised objections to a bunch of criminal thugs moving in, he was badly beaten up and chased out of town. This was the way the gangs conducted business. If you didn't like it, you had your face taken off and put back on the wrong way round. Capone built a big brothel at Forest View. It had huge windows looking out on to the town, so the locals used to say 'Big brothel is watching you'. Al set up base at a hotel in town, although he had to watch that room service wasn't a mouthful of lead. So he had steel shutters added and took other security measures like having the 'Do Not Disturb' sign on the door knob at all times.

When Torrio returned from Italy, he made Al a fifty-fifty partner

*Al often ran classes for people to teach them how to put
their hats on the right way round*

in the business, which was lucky for Al because a lot of gang leaders would have shot him for being too cocky.

Al's main rival, O'Banion, was killed off. Sicilians had a charming custom of rubbing bullets with garlic because they thought it would cause gangrene. It didn't but it made your relatives a bit dubious about kissing you goodbye if you were dying. Mind you, no Sicilian gangster ever got attacked by a vampire.

Eventually Torrio was himself shot and retired from crime because he was too scared. What a big girl's blouse. Al was now in charge and set about securing his empire. At one point all the gangsters were so busy killling each other that for a whole year they didn't have any time to concentrate on their businesses. That's dedication for you.

During Al's reign the first use of a machine gun was recorded. This was very useful because you could kill even more of your rivals in one go. And it made that lovely pop-pop noise as well.

Nicknames were very important and no mobster felt dressed without one. Must have been a bit of a pointer for the coppers, when they were looking for suspects, to be introduced to someone called Machine Gun Kelly.

'He met the press and described himself as an honest businessman. They tried to write this down but couldn't because they were pissing themselves laughing'

Naturally other gangs didn't like Capone being top dog, so they tried to get him. His driver was captured and tortured and there was a massive attack on Capone's men in a restaurant. Capone got a bit indignant and started calling for peace. He met the press and described himself as an honest businessman. They tried to write this down but couldn't because they were pissing themselves laughing.

Al sounded off about lots of things he was unhappy with. Of women he said, 'The trouble with women today is their excitement over too many things outside the home.' Perhaps Mrs Capone was failing to get turned on by washing-up and hoovering any more and had asked to have a go with a machine gun. And that would have been understandable because Al was unfaithful most of the time. His wife would never have found out if it hadn't been for the little matter of a nasty bout of syphilis and the unfortunate situation that nobody had invented antibiotics yet.

Al was responsible for the notorious St Valentine's Day Massacre when seven members of George 'Bugs' Moran's gang were approached by four men, two of whom were wearing police uniform. They expected to be frisked but instead were mown down with machine guns by, among others, Tony 'Big Tuna' Accardo. It was never traced back to Capone but Accardo was subsequently seen in the lobby of Capone's hotel headquarters with a machine gun. This struck people as odd. Normally, of course, he would have been carrying the large fish which gave him his distinctive nickname.

Prohibition made Capone rich. People wanted booze and were prepared to pay for it. Secret drinking dens or speakeasies opened everywhere, just as they have in modern Muslim communities, always owned and controlled by the likes of Capone.

Capone was eventually arrested for tax fraud and ended up in Alcatraz. He passed control of the syndicate to Paul 'The Waiter' Ricca and Frank Nitti. Since Nitti had no nickname he was known as Frank 'No Nickname' Nitti. This was seen as a poor substitute for a proper nickname and it was no surprise when he committed suicide.

By this time Al was on to the ga-ga stage of syphilis and could hear the voice of God. I hope God was giving him a telling off. He was secretly released from prison and died, aged 48, from a heart attack.

Al always got other people to do his dirty work, while he sat in full public view in a restaurant eating clams and looking very dapper in his diamond tie-pin and spats. If it wasn't clams, it was spaghetti. Italian men certainly know how to eat. Pity they don't know how to shag.

MAO
Zedong

Mao forgets the Clearasil on his chin again

'Damn, that spot won't go'

ao Zedong was born in 1893 in a small village in China, the son of a well-off peasant. In those days a well-off peasant had a pair of shoes, an extra goat and an attitude problem.

Mao apparently had a rebellious and restless temperament as an adolescent, but then adolescence is the most unpalatable time of life the world over. If I'd done all the things I'd said I was going to do when I was 14, my parents would be dead, my first boyfriend would be dead and I'd be dead.

In 1911, when Mao was 18, there was a rebellion against the

Ch'ing dynasty who had ruled China since the 17th century. The Chinese were about as keen on this particular dynasty as I was on Dynasty. They had a better reason, though: the Ch'ing dynasty kept them all in grinding poverty. My only reasons were that I hated all those padded shoulders and women taking off their earrings to answer the phone.

After the Ch'ing dynasty was disposed of, China became a republic. Unfortunately the leaders of the revolution couldn't manage to establish a stable government, so civil war broke out and lasted until 1949.

As per usual, women were having a great time while all this was going on. Lots of them had their feet bound, so they walked around like ballet dancers who were dying for the lav and were crap at legging it away from anything scary, like soldiers on the pillage. Feet binding has died out in China now but in the West we women still happily persist in tottering around on a pair of matchsticks. They tilt your womb, they bugger your toes, but don't they look elegant?

As a young man, Mao had trouble deciding which sort of political creed he wanted to follow. He was briefly attracted to constitutional monarchy, so the Chinese peasants might have ended up starving in the fields, but with an unattractive bunch of bejewelled thickos to admire as they snuffed it.

Mao worked in a library in Peking for a while, where he obviously got a taste for saying 'Shh!' a lot and generally polished his skills as a totalitarian dictator. He wasn't happy away from home, though, and kept popping back, especially when he'd run out of clean pants or was fed up with living off Pot Noodles.

Mao was one of the 12 original founders of the Communist Party in China in 1921 and soon emerged as its leader. The country at that time was mainly made up of

'If I'd done all the things I'd said I was going to do when I was 14, my parents would be dead, my first boyfriend would be dead and I'd be dead'

'Mao's legacy to the world is Maoism, like Marxism without the beard'

poverty-stricken, tradition-bound peasants, who knew as much about Communism as they did about Massey-Ferguson tractors.

Mao decided it was time for the peasants to rebel. He went in for some fisticuffs with the Nationalist government but had to flee to mountains with his men. After three years of roaming and regrouping (and nipping home to pick up his clean kecks) he declared a Soviet republic in South-East China. This went down as well as a Page Three model in the Spare Rib office and he was forced to flee to the North-East.

This flight is called the Long March. (The only march in history visible from space.) I don't know how Mao persuaded his men to walk all the way across China. He wouldn't have got me to go further than the first caff. On the Long March personal hygiene was not a priority. Similarly Castro was reputed to have had mice in his beard when fighting in the jungle. Years after the Cuban revolution he found a mouse which thought the war was still going on.

Mao's legacy to the world is Maoism, like Marxism without the beard. He had originally thought that the industrial workers in the cities would be his power base but, when he realised there were only a couple of them and millions of peasants, he changed his mind and concentrated on the peasants. From then on he kept his power base in the countryside. This meant he could hear the birds singing, look at the trees and smell the flowers. Communist dictators don't appreciate these things, however, so China became a totalitarian state and twenty to thirty million were killed in the process. It all started so nicely with happy bands of young Communists distributing food to the peasants. What went wrong? What always goes wrong, sadly. One bloke got a bit of power and started to behave like a knobhead.

Mao tried lots of different schemes to improve the country and gave them silly names like 'The Great Leap Forward'. This

My twin brother

didn't work, probably because most people wanted to try a little hop first. To his followers he may have been God Almighty, emperor and dictator all rolled into one, but he was a man of the people. Although he lived in a palace it wasn't his palace: it was the People's Palace.

Mao also instigated The Cultural Revolution. This was a bad time for intellectuals: the lucky ones got their heads kicked in; the rest were executed. You had to be really careful to come last in the pub quiz. Mao was very busy at this time writing 2,300 publications on his own special theories of Communism. He had to make deliberate spelling mistakes so people didn't think he was too much of a clever bastard, otherwise he would have had to have himself executed.

Mao was helped in his quest for absolute power by the Red Guard, a uniformed militia of youthful, shrieking zealots who terrorised the intellectuals like an hysterical gestapo. There was no pretence of legality. Suspects were dragged into the street, beaten with sticks, interrogated and tortured. If that didn't work, they were criticised. This was Mao's secret weapon. He even invited people to criticise him and, when they did, he had them killed. Eventually everybody said everything was great, even Mao's name.

The Great Helmsman is now long gone but at the time of writing his successor Deng Xiaoping is still hanging on to power, thanks to the occasional large espresso and a couple of thousand volts. The rest of the world were so outraged by the massacre that took place in Tiananmen Square under his command that they stopped talking to the Chinese (for about ten minutes).

Chinese are born entrepreneurs and, by suppressing this instinct for so long, Mao may have achieved the opposite of what he intended: when Communism eventually does collapse, China is going to explode in an orgy of capitalism that will make the Japanese look like hippies.

Mao comes last in the London to Brighton Rally

MIKHAIL
Gorbachev

The best known pate in the business

Blue Peter badge winner 1991

orby (for that sadly is what the press have dubbed him, along with an inability on the part of commentators to avoid adding a Y to the end of every footballer in the world. Pity they don't put it at the beginning of the name because most footballers are just big Y-fronts as far as I'm concerned) was born in 1931 in Stavropol and his childhood coincided with Stalin's reign of terror. In fact his grandad spent nine years in prison camps, poor sod, probably for picking his nose.

Gorby was too young for the war, unlike my brother's father-in-law, Helmut the German, who was in a Russian prisoner-of-war camp until five years after the war. He recalls the Russians as very friendly and naive. When the Germans put on plays for the locals, the German officers would play the female parts because they had longer hair. The Russian soldiers would be open-mouthed with amazement and say to the Germans after the play, 'Where did you get those women from?'

I don't think Gorby was quite that naive. He was a swot at school and joined Komsomol, the young Communists group. Not quite full-blown Reds, they were more sort of Pinky and Perky. Gorby's stunning educational record gave him the opportunity to be a combine-harvester driver for four years. Less able pupils had to clean the combine harvester with a toothbrush.

'Not quite full-blown Reds, they were more sort of Pinky and Perky'

Gorby eventually got away from this and managed to get a place at Moscow State University, where he studied law and joined the Communist Party. He also met Raisa there and married her and they have one child. Raisa is the nearest thing the Russians have to Liz Taylor. Gorby can't afford diamonds but I believe he gives her the occasional banana. He returned to Stavropol and rose through the Party bureaucracy and in 1980 became a member of the Politburo, the ruling body of Russia. This was during the Brezhnev years. Russian politics then was a bit like the judiciary over here. The top dogs went on for ever, well after their sell-by date, in fact almost as if they were counting their ages in dog years. Many Russian leaders were so old that they could remember when they were treated like shit by royalty, instead of by Stalin.

During the reigns of Andropov and Chernenko Gorby became a prominent member of the Party and, when Chernenko snuffed it at the age of 537, Gorby succeeded him, surprising the rest of the world because he could still feed himself, get around without the aid of a bathchair and didn't feel an irresistible compulsion to go round telling people how

Michail Gorbachev

'Smile, Capitalist Swine'

old he was. Gorby got power by a very small margin. He was up against someone called Grishkin, who was a real conservative. Think how different it could have been. Yeah, lucky Muscovites might have been able to avoid getting a McDonald's, being overrun by the Mafia and managing a crime rate higher than that in Washington.

It's strange how a woman has never got to the top in Russia as there seems to be much less discrimination towards them there. They could always be doctors, drive lorries and work on the land but I'm sure they still managed to hang on to traditional female roles like cooking dinner, doing a bit of ironing and being knocked about by their old men.

Gorby travelled abroad quite a lot so he knew what a pair of Levis looked like. He set about making lots of changes and was responsible for the rest of the world learning a bit of Russian in the two words *peristroika* and *glasnost*. Up to this point the only Russian words the rest of the world knew were 'vodka' and 'Reds under the bed'. Most of those who were

Jo Brand – A Load of Old Balls

paranoid about Russia invading actually had only potties under their beds.

Glasnost means 'openness' and allowed Russia to tell people a bit more about what was going on. It also meant Russians for the first time in ages could criticise the government. Why they'd worried about it for so long I don't know. If one or two people criticising the government made any difference, the only leader people would agree on would be Mr Blobby.

Perestroika means reconstruction. So was Gorby one of the first reconstructed men? Dunno, 'cause I've never seen a reconstructed man, apart from the six-million-dollar man... and all those super powers meant he would just be able to leg it out of my bedroom quicker.

The tabloid press does tend to reduce things to superficial appearances and much was made of Gorby's birthmark. Let's be honest, though, if a woman had had that, she'd never have got out of the front door without a bag on her head. In sign language, the short-cut symbol for Gorby is a tap on the front of the head. Not very PC, is it? Still it's an improvement on the sign for Ronald Reagan, which is just a big dribble.

Russia began to have free (-ish) elections and all the countries it had governed or tried to, up to that point, started to break away. The last of the hold-outs was Romania, led by Ceausescu and his wife, the Psycho Darby and Joan of world politics, who were executed. I've been to Romania and it's nice to see their knowledge of politics is no better than ours. When I told a cab driver I was English he said, 'Ah! Sam Fox.' Bloody depressing, innit?

322

Michail Gorbachev

Gorbachev met many world leaders, including Reagan whose world view was shallow and cartoon like. The Americans were developing a satellite which would, theoretically, pick off Soviet missiles before they could hit a target. Reagan called it Star Wars because that was the name of a movie. He picked it at random. It could just as easily have been called Lassie Come Home or The Blob.

With the new freedoms it didn't take long for the Russians wholeheartedly to embrace such Western staples as unemployment. They even came up with their own cannibal serial killer. No one can accuse them of not making the effort.

Hard-line Commies were not happy with Gorby and tried a *coup d'état*. This collapsed but Gorby resigned anyway. It was really only a matter of time before he adopted Boris Yeltsin's position – flat on his back with a bottle of vodka in his mouth.

Gorby was very popular with the Western world and not surprisingly as they were looking around for a big country to exploit. Unfortunately he was not so popular at home because the paradise people thought would come has been put on hold.

And now he is gone we are faced with bumbling Boris the Hooligan. Russia is rotting and the hotbed of greed that is now the Moscow criminal network threatens all our safety. Materials for nuclear weapons are available if you've got the money. This has been uncovered by a brave hero. It's not someone from MI6, though. It's good old Roger Cook. Roger, could you go and get Gorby back for us?

323

Frank
Sinatra

Frank always closed one eye when he was pissed so he could see the microphone

*Frank points out someone
he hasn't slept with*

rank Sinatra was a mummy's boy. His mother was well-known for using foul language and so was he. Mind you, he weighed 13 pounds when he was born, so I'm not really surprised she swore. Anything to help him squeeze his way out a bit easier.

Frank's dad was a fireman and his mum a midwife who did the odd illegal abortion on the side. Always nice to have a hobby.

Frank's rise to fame started when he joined a group whom he had been pestering to let him in for ages. They were called

The Three Flashes. What a pity they didn't have an 'R' on the end of their name. They didn't want Frank in but he went whining to his mum and she sorted it out for him.

> **'Frank's dad was a fireman and his mum a midwife who did the odd illegal abortion on the side. Always nice to have a hobby'**

Irritatingly for the guys in the group, Frank turned out to be the best singer and would be besieged by girls backstage. This was the earliest example of three blokes being tangoed.

Frank's mother wanted Frank to get married and, even though he didn't want to, he agreed to it to please his old mum. He married a girl called Nancy Barbato and made a point of saying to her, 'I'm going to the top I don't want anyone dragging on my neck.' Strangely, this didn't evoke the response 'Piss off then, mummy's boy' and Nancy blithely stepped into the most unappealing future until Mandy Smith said 'I do' to Bill Wyman.

Frank began to get decent work and was offered a two-year contract with the Harry James band. (In those days you didn't have to be too imaginative about the name of your band.)

Frank was always competitive and would have fights with other members of the band about being in the limelight.

He was also starting to be unfaithful and, like many a sad old bastard on his way to the top, he started having an affair with a blonde starlet. He wanted to divorce Nancy but his mummy wouldn't let him, so

> **'His mother became an admired member of the Red Cross and started saying "Gracious me!" instead of "Bollocks!"'**

naughty Frank just carried on behind her back.

A bloke called George Evans took over Frank's publicity and hired girls to go to his concerts and scream. He also created a

You can take your glasses off Ava.
He's sitting on what he thinks the sun shines out of

new biography for Frank and his family, leaving out the unpalatable bits. His mother became an admired member of the Red Cross and started saying 'Gracious me!' instead of 'Bollocks!'

Frank was a man's man who had a passion for boxing. He liked to watch it and he also quite liked to punch people himself from time to time. He had a very bad temper and enjoyed belittling people, although this was quite hard for him because he was small and scrawny.

When Frank went to MGM to make films he pinned a list of actresses on his door that he wanted to shag. He worked his way through the list but, when his mum came to visit, he had to say they were just autographs he wanted for her.

Frank fell passionately in love with the actress Ava Gardner and eventually married her. Their relationship was beset with problems because Ava would not put up with crap. Frank constantly accused Ava of having affairs, which she would have been doing if she'd had any sense.

Meanwhile poor old Nancy was trying to get him back. She is quoted as saying about Ava, 'What can she do for him in bed that I can't do?' Hmm, that shows a mature understanding of relationships, doesn't it?

'Frank constantly accused Ava of having affairs, which she would have been doing if she'd had any sense'

Ava was nicknamed 'The Man' because she was so combative and aggressive but everyone reckoned this was just down to the insecurity she had that she couldn't hang on to a man. Sadly, as women, all our motives are re-interpreted in relation to men. Apparently I must be a lesbian because I have a go at blokes and I'm not beautiful. Even poor old lesbians are only lesbians because they can't get a bloke. In fact men could find a reason to say all women are lesbians if they tried hard enough, and where would that leave them?

Frank's marriage with Ava broke up and he slashed his wrists. At least it kept him from slashing anyone else's for a while. At this point women flocked to try to sort him out. Judy Garland wanted to marry him. He chucked her. Liz Taylor got pregnant by him. He arranged an abortion. No one was having much luck.

He had an affair with Lauren Bacall and eventually proposed to her. She made the mistake of telling everyone and Frank was promptly besieged by the Press. He told Lauren they would have to lie low for a while and didn't talk to her for six years. I expect she considered herself well and truly chucked by that time.

Anyone who criticised Frank was in big trouble even if he was a friend. Sammy Davis Junior once said in an interview that Frank could be rude and treat people like shit. Frank called him 'a dirty nigger bastard' and dropped him from a film. So at least Sammy had the satisfaction of knowing he was right.

Frank could be racist. He called Count Basie's orchestra 'a

chess set'. But he thought that was all right because he had black friends.

Frank always hated the press and would go bonkers if he was given a bad review. Having encountered a woman journalist who had been nasty about him he announced to the assembled group that a certain part of her smelt very bad. (Not her armpits.) Frank then asked one of his minions to buy up as many vaginal deodorants as he could and send them to her. The man's wit and sophistication is astounding, isn't it? I wonder what mum would have thought about this little escapade. The mum deodorant connection was never made as Frank kept his nasty petty little tantrums to himself by then.

Frank also married Mia Farrow who was an old hippy whereas Frank was just old. Frank didn't want Mia to work and so that marriage broke up as well. Mia went on to marry Woody Allen and prove how much of a hippy she was by calling her son Satchel.

Frank's life has been full of intrigues. He has been accused of consorting with the Mafia and was also involved, people think, in trying to silence the comic Jackie Mason who made jokes about him and Mia.

Frank certainly did it 'his way'. It's a pity that it was the way of a petulant, chauvinistic, puerile little kid. The lady was obviously a tramp because she'd rather live in a cardboard box than hang about waiting for Frank to humiliate her.

I've finished.
Can you wheel me off now?

331

ROBIN
Hood

Robin caught cross-dressing by a local redneck

Robin always had the horn

o one really knows whether Robin Hood existed or not. He's a bit like Father Christmas, but
with a social conscience. Robin robbed the rich (the clergy)
and gave to the poor (everybody else). A dispossessed noble-
man, he pledged allegiance to King Richard, who was busy at
the crusades trying to keep Jerusalem British.

Most of the knowledge we have about Robin Hood is
gleaned from medieval ballads which aren't famed for their
accuracy. They were the pop songs of their time, so most of
them are full of utter nonsense about lurve.

There are several theories as to Robin's identity including the

335

possibility that he was the Earl of Huntingdon, that he was a Yorkshireman or, my personal theory, that he was a sort of 12th-century social worker who turned violent because of the poor performance record of Nottingham Forest FC.

'Go to any disco on a Friday night and you can see at least one drunk woman "doing a Friar Tuck" as she comes out of the toilet'

Of course one theory is that Robin never existed but is a mythical figure related to the Green Man, a sort of woodland spirit with leaves growing round his head. The legend of the Green Man also spawned morris dancers, so it is a very unwelcome legend indeed.

The most famous ballad about Robin is called *The Gest of Robin Hood* and describes various adventures that Robin had with the gang he hung around with. They included Friar Tuck who was, of course, the fat bloke who ate like a horse but was dead good at fighting. Sadly it is thought that he did not get his name from spending too much time at the Tuck Shop, but from tucking his dress into his belt. Go to any disco on a Friday night and you can see at least one drunk woman 'doing a Friar Tuck' as she comes out of the toilet.

In one famous story Robin asks Friar Tuck to take him across the ford and he refuses, so they have a fight. During the fight Tuck's dogs catch arrows in their mouths. Unlikely, as the only dogs hard enough to do that are Rottweilers and I don't think they were around then. Perhaps the legend just fails to tell us that the dogs got killed in the process.

Robin Hood was the best shot in England with a longbow. He would often turn up at archery tournaments in disguise and deliberately miss the target in case the authorities realised who he was and arrested him. Yeah, Gazza uses that excuse when he misses too. According to the well-known song Hood was feared by the bad and loved by the good, but this was only because it rhymed with his name. He was also fond of riding through the glen, so he obviously spent a lot of time in Scotland. Being a bit of a hard man, Robin must have really resented his parents for giving him a bird's name. His sister, Little Red Riding, was

'His sister, Little Red Riding, was named after a small but particularly left-wing part of Yorkshire'

named after a small but particularly left-wing part of Yorkshire.

Robin's gang included Will Scarlet, so named because he was very embarrassed about having to wear tights, Alan A Dale, a minstrel recently honoured by having a packet of little chocolates named after him, and Little John. Little John was named ironically, because he is supposed to have been seven-foot tall. I think lots of Americans were very confused to see him portrayed as a big bloke in *Robin, Prince of Thieves*, as their grasp of irony isn't too hot.

Together these 'merry men' dined every night on venison. Of course, hunting the King's deer carried the death penalty, as did rabbit rustling, reciting the Lord's Prayer backwards and looking at people in a funny way, and there were gibbets at every crossroads. So, to avoid detection Robin dressed his men in Lincoln Green, which was great camouflage until autumn came.

Robin's arch enemy was the Sheriff of Nottingham, who kept a falcon on his wrist, a raven on his shoulder and schemed his evil schemes to uphold the law, protect travellers from interference and bring robbers to justice. Sounds like a right bastard. The poor loved Hood and he is still an extremely popular figure, although today he'd be doing thirty years in Parkhurst.

With any hero there has to be a love interest, and Robin's was Maid Marian, who looked exactly like Michelle Pfeiffer and spent her time swooning in various towers and being in danger of being ravished by baddies. Robin always rescued her but must have got quite frustrated as 'maid' in those days meant virgin and Marian never changed her name to Unmaid Marian.

Robin met his death in a very unpleasant way.

'Look, Maid Marian, you've got the right body for a supermodel but sort out the facial hair'

He went to stay with a relative, who was an abbess, and she bled him until he snuffed it. Perhaps the family inheritance was a biggie or he'd given away her best cutlery to some poor people down the road.

'hunting the King's deer carried the death penalty, as did rabbit rustling, reciting the Lord's Prayer backwards and looking at people in a funny way'

Just before he died, Robin managed to fire an arrow and was buried where it landed. I'm crap at archery, so if I tried that I'd have to be buried under my settee. It's about time someone like Robin Hood came along today and reversed the process that's going on in Britain today. All we've got is Major and his band of jolly grey men, robbing the poor to give to the rich. I'd have a go myself but I look crap in green.

Still, I might audition for the Friar Tuck part.

Due to the lack of women, many of Robin's men proposed to horses

RASPUTIN
Ra! Ra!

A rare photo of Rasputin with the two
members of the Russian
population he never shagged

*Rasputin finally flipped when he was pipped
to the Doctor Who job by Tom Baker*

asputin lived from about 1872 to 1916 and
his real name was Grigori Efimovitch Rasputin
was a nickname which means 'debauchee'. Bit of a giveaway if
he was hoping to get lots of invitations to Sunday School tea
parties.

Rasputin was born of peasant parents in Western Siberia and
received no education at all. But when has that ever stopped
a mad monk trying to take over the world? (The fact that
Rasputin wasn't a monk or diagnosed as mad is neither here
nor there.)

Rasputin was a bit clever and possessed a magnetic personality, although this could be explained by the fact that he may

have used hypnotism. I should think it's highly likely. From his photos the man looks like a heavy metal fan with rabies, so he would be your first choice to chat up at the disco.

'hair greasy enough to fry an egg on, eyes that would have been at home in Marty Feldman's face and a tunic that could make it back to Siberia on its own'

As a young man Rasputin joined a sect known as the Khlysty or 'flagellants' and decided he was a miracle worker. Notice that verb 'decided' there. I don't think he'd quite got the hang of the miracle worker concept. You can't 'decide' yourself – you have to make a few warts disappear or deal with a nasty cough – just as you can't 'decide' you are a fabulous person whom everyone loves, although Za Za Gabor seems to have got round that problem.

In particular Rasputin preached that intimate physical contact with his own body could cure people, particularly women of course. Well I never. I'm surprised more people haven't tried this approach. It's cheaper than joining Dateline.

Rasputin was accused of heresy at this time, but got off the charge. Perhaps he slipped the judge a length.

Soon Rasputin decided that local women weren't enough for him and he wanted to expand. He thought he might as well head straight for the top, so he made his way to St Petersburg, where Tsar Nicholas lived, and wormed his way into the society of Orthodox aristocrats.

At the time there was a wave of belief in mysticism. This was very handy because it meant Rasputin could say any old cobblers he wanted and they would all believe him. People are still very superstitious today about things and you will find lots of performers have silly little rituals they go through before a show to ensure they do well. One of my silly little rituals before a show used to be drinking eight pints of lager. This would only ensure that I wanted to fight the audience, though.

'If you don't smile I'll shag you all again'

Because the upper classes in St Petersburg didn't have a problem with hair greasy enough to fry an egg on, eyes that would have been at home in Marty Feldman's face and a tunic that could make it back to Siberia on its own, Rasputin was soon surrounded by an adoring gaggle of upper-class women devotees, most of whom he shafted with gusto. I can't help thinking it serves them right. I know Princess Di hasn't got the world record for O Levels but even she hasn't sloped off for a dirty weekend with David Icke on Planet Bonkers.

Rasputin met the Empress Alexandra in 1905 and she was 'smitten by him'. What was the matter with these women? It's not as though there weren't any eligible blokes around and, compared to Rasputin, a book about scaffolding would have been a suitable alternative.

What really cracked it for Rasputin with the Empress was the fact that her son Alexis, who was a haemophiliac, seemed to get better when Rasputin was around. Many times when the doctors had given up hope Rasputin would pray and the child would recover. Maybe the poor kid was so terrified he didn't dare bleed.

345

Jo Brand – A Load of Old Balls

Emperor Nicholas went along with his wife, who decided Rasputin was a saint sent from heaven. She didn't take into account that most saints have a level of hygiene above that of a teenage boy whose parents have gone on holiday for a fortnight. And they don't try to shag you, either.

Rasputin gradually began to poke his nose into matters of state, which were very dodgy at the time, given that the revolutionaries were on the brink of taking over.

Through Rasputin Nicholas came to believe he was in touch with the ordinary Russian masses, although in fact he was about as in touch with them as John Major is with the English masses, ordinary as he is. This caused big rows between Nick and the government, and you can see their point really. There they were happily handing out their orders and then along comes this jumped-up nutter in a dirty dress who not only seems a more attractive proposition to their wives but is half-cut all the time and smells like a compost heap where a bunch of elephants with flatulence live.

A rumour spread quickly that the Empress and her daughters were among Rasputin's many mistresses, which apparently was not true. It seems nausea may have prevented them from taking the plunge.

Not surprisingly Rasputin's hypnotic power over the Empress caused lots of resentment and he became the subject of such virulent dinner-party gossip that hostesses were forced to put up signs saying 'We do not talk about Rasputin here'.

During the war Nicholas ignored domestic affairs, which were left totally in the hands of Alexandra and Rasputin. Corruption was rife, with appointments being bought and sold, and Rasputin continued his debauchery, or 'rasputing', safely guarded by secret police agents.

Rasputin's meddling helped to widen the gulf between Nicholas and the masses. Eventually a bunch of right-wingers could take it no more and a group of high-ranking conservatives assassinated him in December 1916. Happy Christmas, Rasp.

The murder itself was sordid, Rasputin being unsuccessfully poisoned, then shot. In all the films, just to make it more exciting, we see these conservatives try even more different methods like drowning, strangulation, stabbing, garrotting and a double dose of Head and Shoulders. For those of you that don't think I've quite made it on the academic front with my portrayal of Rasputin, I would refer you to the single by 70s band Boney M, which has the immortal line:

'Ra Ra Rasputin, Russia's greatest love machine.'

Pure Shakespeare.

GEORGE
Orwell

George working for the Big Bad Communists

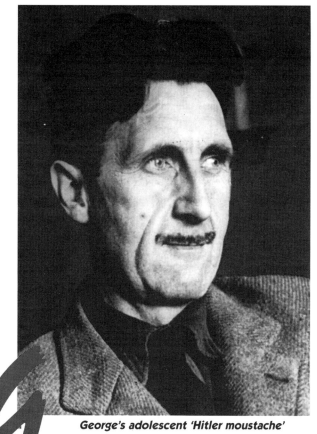

George's adolescent 'Hitler moustache'
experiment lasted well into his 40s

eorge Orwell's real name was Eric Blair and his father was a junior officer in the Opium Department in India. Eric's father married late to an up-market French woman called Ida Limouzin. She had a French father but was born in Penge. That's a bit like having a boyfriend who's a pop star and then having to tell everyone it's Mr Blobby.

Eric was one of three children and they had a cosy middle-class upbringing after they moved into a house in Henley called Nutshell.

Eric was a lonely, isolated child, which is very good training for being a writer as most writers aren't very jolly. Cheerful people don't make very good writers because they write things like 'Everything is very nice'.

'That's a bit like having a boyfriend who's a pop star and then having to tell everyone it's Mr Blobby'

Eric's brother-in-law described him as 'a nasty fat little boy with a constant grievance'. I'm not surprised, given that he was sent away at the age of eight to a boarding school in Eastbourne. The place made Eric very unhappy and he became a bedwetter. The headmistress of the school had a very caring approach to the problems of lonely little boys. She beat them. Depressing as it might be, this actually worked for Eric and the bedwetting stopped.

Eric's later socialist leanings were beginning to form at this school. He noticed that rich kids were treated much better than scholarship kids like him. When they wet the bed they were made prefects and promised a job in the Civil Service.

Little Eric went on to Eton but never really shone academically doing just enough to get by. He is described at this stage as having 'a fat face and long jowls like a hamster'. Poor old Eric obviously wasn't up to much in the looks department, but that didn't matter as he was a man, so people didn't care what he looked like.

After Eton the normal route would have been Oxford or Cambridge for Eric the Hamster. However, he decided against this and applied to join a police training scheme in Burma. Eric sailed to Burma and, as he disembarked, saw a clumsy coolie being kicked by a policeman. What really wound Eric up was the look of smug satisfaction on all the posh English people's faces as they came off the ship. This is the same look you can see on the upper classes' faces today as they think about their money and how many poor people are being ground into the dirt for them to get it.

Eric described his experience in Burma as 'five years within the sound of bugles'. He might have described Eton as 'five years within the sound of buggery'.

'One of the problems he had was that he could not spell rude words and she must have laughed sadly to herself as she looked at one of his stories, *Rich People Are Fokking Prates*'

By this point Eric was an anti-imperialist, although he couldn't stand being sneered at by Buddhist monks and local Burmese. Obviously he forgot he had a policeman's uniform on and that, however nice a policeman he may be, for lots of people seeing someone in that uniform is the equivalent of seeing someone wearing a shell suit – it makes you want to slap them.

Eric returned to the UK at the age of twenty-four and moved back in with his parents. Before very long he was getting on everyone's nerves. He never tidied his room and mooned about the whole time. So he moved out and went to London to become a writer.

He began by writing poetry, which according to his friend Miss Pitter was crap. She suggested he tried prose. He wrote short stories. Sadly these were crap too.

One of the problems he had was that he could not spell rude words and she must have laughed sadly to herself as she looked at one of his stories, *Rich People Are Fokking Prates*.

In despair Miss Pitter suggested Eric wrote about what he knew. Hey presto, it worked and George Orwell was born.

George began putting on rags and going into the East End to see how the poor people lived. Lots of people could tell he was quite posh, though, probably because he wasn't very good at saying rude words either.

George then decided that to be a writer you have to go to Paris, so off he went. He wrote two novels there which were rejected, so he destroyed them. (*Inherited Wealth is Crape*

Jo Brand – A Load of Old Balls

and *Why I Hate Right-Wing Barstids.*)

Orwell said his worst experience in Paris was being hospitalised with pneumonia, when two nurses buckled him into an agonising mustard poltice. I don't know what this was, but he got better, the moaning old git.

George ran out of money and was forced to be a washer-upper in a hotel. This is the first recorded incident ever of an Englishman doing the washing-up.

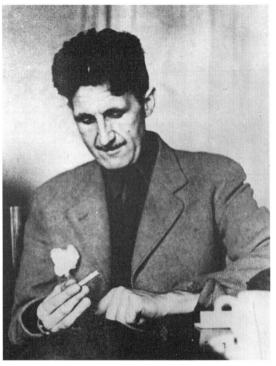

George gets to grip with the new fun-shaped female condom

Orwell was obviously worn out by this and went back to his family in England. He decided he wanted to see what prison was like, so got very drunk and was arrested. The police gave him a cup of tea and let him go the next day, so that was very disappointing for him.

His novel, *Animal Farm*, was rejected by several publishers, one of whom suggested the pigs should be changed to nicer creatures to soothe the Kremlin. Animal Farm led by a group of gerbils might have been nice.

'George ran out of money and was forced to be a washer-upper in a hotel. This is the first recorded incident ever of an Englishman doing the washing-up'

354

Orwell went to Spain and supported the Republicans in the Spanish Civil War, then returned to England to write some of his greatest works. He had been working with soldiers, so by now he had learned how to say rude words properly, but not necessarily spell them correctly.

Orwell's work has had a tremendous effect on contemporary literature, bringing new words and phrases into the language such as Big Brother, Newspeak and wankkere.

In 1984 the *Daily Mail* serialised *Nineteen Eighty-Four.* How clever of them. Funnily enough they left out a section describing entertainment to keep the proles happy including 'rubbishy newspapers containing almost nothing except sport, crime and astrology'. Oh dear, George, you left out 'petty suburban right-wing values'.

A very stark vision of the future, *Nineteen Eighty-Four* asks us to imagine 'a boot stamping on a face forever'.

A boot stamping on the *Daily Mail* forever would be a good start for me.

JACK
The Ripper

Vidal Sassoon's early method's were not appreciated by his customers

The most boring picture in this book

nappetising as this character is, I have decided to have a look at him because his existence illustrates very well, even today, the attitude to murderers of his ilk, whose victims are women.

First of all, he had a nickname, which I think is a bit odd for a psycho who goes round mutilating women. Nicknames tend to be given to people we are fond of. Nobody was fond of Jack the Ripper, apart from the Press because a good murder sells papers.

Jack the Ripper, whoever he was, badly mutilated his victims, all of whom happened to be prostitutes. Somehow everyone seemed to feel it wasn't quite so bad to murder women who had sex for money, because that was obviously an occupational hazard. Even today you will find judges using phrases like 'contributory negligence' or 'she was asking for it', about women who display any tendencies towards loose morals, which lets the bloke off the hook. Even walking around with a short skirt on is considered by some members of the judiciary to be 'asking for it'. So hockey players had better watch out as they have only themselves to blame if they are attacked. Cheerleaders, on the other hand, deserve anything they get.

Theories abound as to the identity of Jack the Ripper but the most famous one involves a plot to cover up the sexual misdemeanours of a member of the Royal Family. They are not quite so easy to cover up these days owing to the profusion of sad radio ham types listening in to people's conversations, hoping they'll get lucky with a 'Squidgy' tape. I'm sure

'in those days, it was considered scandalous to be unmarried and pregnant. It's the same today, but only if you get a council flat'

most of them only ever hear the interminable conversations of businessmen: calls to the wife about being home late for dinner, followed by calls to the secretary to arrange to meet at a hotel, followed by calls to the wife to say they love her, followed by calls to the secretary to say they're leaving the wife, followed by calls to the wife to say 'Happy Birthday', followed by calls to the secretary to say, 'You're sacked; you forgot the flowers.'

The main theory about Jack the Ripper's identity involves Prince Albert Victor, Duke of Clarence, who was Queen Victoria's grandson. He got to know an artist called Sickert who led a very Bohemian life. (In Victorian times that meant he didn't have his dinner on the table at six o'clock on the dot. He may even have gone as far as having his dinner on his lap.) Supposedly the Duke of Clarence, or 'Eddy' as he was known, had an affair with a woman who lived near Sickert, called Annie Crook. She became pregnant and gave birth to a royal bastard. (I didn't realise you had to be unmarried to give birth to a royal bastard.) This came to the attention of the Prime Minister, Lord Salisbury, who, along with other posh people, was worried that the monarchy was in jeopardy because of the rise of Socialism and, feeling the royal philandering might not go down too well with the masses, decided to sort things out.

Annie Crook was kidnapped and ended up in a lunatic asylum. So did lots of other women who got pregnant in those days, because it was considered scandalous to be unmarried and pregnant. It's the same today, but only if you get a council flat.

Marie Kelly, a woman who was looking after the baby, escaped with the kid back to the East End and got in with some prostitutes, whom she told about what had gone on. Well, you'd have to have a gossip about something like that. It's better than finding out your next-door neighbour's taking half an hour to pay the milk bill.

Artist's impressions weren't any better in those days

Worried that these women would blow the gaff, Salisbury decided to sort them out and used William Gull, a royal physician, to murder anyone who knew about the scandal. It is believed it was a Masonic plot which the Royal Family knew nothing about, but involved a high-ranking policeman called Sir Robert Anderson. Not like the police to be involved in that sort of thing, is it?

The problem with this theory is that it's such a long time ago and all the people who were involved have snuffed it. Some people think Sickert the artist could have been the murderer, others think it was someone called the Mad Pork Butcher or even Sherlock Holmes, although he didn't even exist.

At one point Scotland Yard were receiving a thousand letters a week about it, most of them from cranks. It's a pity that this society is so full of cranks who get involved any time there is a major crime.Even when Baby Abbie was kidnapped some bloke kept phoning to say his wife had her. When he was arrested, he was allowed one phone call. He telephoned his lawyer and told him his house was on fire.

Because the Jack the Ripper murders happened such a long time ago, it is now considered acceptable to use them as entertainment and tourists flock to find out all the grotesque details of what he got up to. But then one of the most popular films of recent years has involved a cannibal trying to catch a criminal who is kidnapping women and mutilating them. It's great to be a woman, isn't it?